DOUG LINDSTRAND'S
ALASKA SKETCHBOOK

Sourdough Studio
www.sourdoughstudio.com

Twelfth Revised Sketchbook Edition

Alaska Sketchbook

Copyright © 2008 Douglas W. Lindstrand

ISBN 978-1-928722-04-5
12th U.S. Edition, April, 2008

Publisher: Sourdough Studio
Computer Layout: Mary Humphrey
Printed in Korea
Printing and binding through:
AIPEX.com, Seattle, WA.

All art and photographs by author.

   This book, Alaska Sketchbook, may not be reproduced in whole or in part, by mimeograph, photo process, any electronic or mechanical device, or by any other means, without permission from the publisher.

   Also, because a main purpose of this Sketchbook is to acquaint the reader with Alaska's magnificent wildlife, the author chose to use a few "better" animal photos that were taken "outside" or in captivity.

Red Fox

** Book Orders** : Please contact your favorite bookstore.
   Or: Sourdough Studio, PO Box 92205, Anchorage, AK., 99509   www.sourdoughstudio.com
                                                                                   Info@sourdoughstudio.com

   To order an <u>autographed</u> copy of this book, please send check or money order for the cover price plus $6 shipping. *Include any "special" autographing requests.* **<u>Also, original art and photographic prints are available on request.</u>**

<u>Other books by author: (ISBN 10's and/or 13's)</u>

"Wild Alaska" (hardcover) ISBN 1-928722-00-8 or ISBN 978-1-928722-01-4   ($29.95 cover price)
"Drawing Mammals" ISBN 1-56523-141-4   ($25 cover price)
"Deer: The Ultimate Artist's Reference" ISBN 1-56523-195-3   ($19.95 cover price)
"Bear: The Ultimate Artist's Reference" ISBN 1-56523-214-3   ($19.95 cover price)
"The Artist's Guide to Drawing Realistic Animals" ISBN 1-58180-728-7   ($19.99 cover price)
"Mountain Royalty" (hardcover) ISBN 1-928722-02-4 or ISBN 978-1-928722-02-1   ($29.95 cover price)

   <u>Currently "sold out"</u>:

   "Drawing Big Game" ISBN 1-56523-140-6
   "Drawing America's Wildlife" ISBN 1-56523-203-8

Grizzly

Wolf

Bald Eagle

In the summer of 1970 I began an *adventure*. That adventure was a trek north to America's "Last Frontier" and to there study the wildlife that roamed its legendary and magnificent country.

From the tiny lemming of the Alaskan tundra to the huge, graceful whales of the frigid arctic seas, I wanted to see and learn about them all. To hike up into the high country in spring to watch the Dall lambs at play; to canoe down wild stretches of river to film the magnificent grizzly fishing his favorite stretch of water during the summer's salmon runs; to lean up against a tree on a crisp autumn eve and listen to the lonely cry of a loon on some distant pond. And then, when the winters would come with their cold and snow, I would fly out to some remote "bush" cabin to paint and draw, using the notes, photographs and field-sketches accumulated during the preceding warmer months as my reference as well as inspiration. In short, I would try in my own style to somehow record this continuing adventure of the North Country.

And so it was. I did most of this and more, and from my first meeting with *her* I have been in love with this Grand Lady, Alaska. Land of the Eskimo, Denali, wolf packs and the dazzling Northern Lights. Land of awesome, seemingly barren stretches of tundra, thousands of miles of coastland, sourdoughs and gold. A land teeming with countless miles of virgin streams and of mountains and meadows that no man has ever climbed or walked through. A land big enough for a restless and curious man to stretch his legs in; a land where he can follow his own rainbow and reach for his own chosen stars. A land I now proudly call home.

I would like to dedicate this book to my Mom and Dad, who gave me the opportunity, faith and inspiration to pursue my *Alaskan adventure*. Also, a heartfelt thanks to America's Armed Forces, whose courage, sacrifice and dedication protects and ensures our cherished freedoms.

INTRODUCTION

This "Alaska Sketchbook" is the condensation of hundreds of field-sketches, studio-drawn sketches, photographs and paintings. It is a diary of sorts, a journal of my years of wanderings and contacts with the wildlife, wilderness and people of the North.

During these exciting years as an Alaskan I have seen, studied, and/or drawn almost every game bird, bird of prey, fish, and mammal of interior Alaska (by saying "interior" means exclusive of the coastal waters. I have not yet seen all the different species of whales – many being rare or endangered – that ply Alaska's frigid coastal waters.) Someday I hope to say that I have known *ALL* of Nature's Alaskan children.

Although my main intent of this sketchbook was to better familiarize the viewer with Alaska's favorite treasure - its *magnificent wildlife* - I have also tried to package it into somewhat of an instructional booklet for those not only interested in wildlife but also in drawing, painting and/or photographing it. Many of the birds and mammals have been shown in various poses to better help portray the species to the novice artist; those needing such reference for help in their particular craft (woodcarving, painting, taxidermy, etc.). Also, I have added a section on "Alaskans", as without these fascinating people no book on Alaska would be complete.

This particular Alaska Sketchbook is the Twelfth Revised Edition. Over the years I have added new photos and art and have continued the journal entries regarding my life as an artist. It has also been named Alaska*n* Sketchbook during these preceding twelve editions and has been both self-published and published by others. I guess it could rightfully be called an "*Alaskan Best-seller*" since well over 150,000 Sketchbooks have been sold. And, although I have now written and illustrated numerous other art and Alaskan books, it is still my personal "*favorite*". It is, after all, a condensed summation of my Alaska life story; an artist's adventure here in America's magnificent "Last Frontier".

I hope you enjoy.

Willow Ptarmigan / Autumn Colors

INDEX

1-5………..Introduction pages
6-33……...."**Alaskans**"
34……...…"**Birds of Alaska**"
35-44…......Eagles, Hawks & Falcons
45-55…......Owls
56-59…......Grouse
60-63…......Ptarmigan
64-67…......Canada Geese
68-70….......Other Alaska Geese
71-76…......Ducks
77-79…......Loons & Swans
80-81…......Sandhill Crane
82-86…......Assorted Birds
87-89….......Puffins
90………..."**Mammals of Alaska**"
91-102…...Dall Sheep
103-109…Moose
110-120…Caribou
121-131…Brown Bear / Grizzly
132-136…Black Bear
137-141…Polar Bear
142-144…Roosevelt Elk
145-147…Sitka Black-Tailed Deer
148-149…Bison
150-153…Mountain Goat
154-155…Muskox
156-163…Wolf
164-165…Coyote
166-170…Red Fox
171-173…Arctic Fox
174-175…Lynx
176-177…Wolverine
178-179…Walrus
180-183…Seals & Otters
184-185…Porcupine
186-187…Snowshoe Hare
188-193…Small Mammals
194-199…Whales, Fish & Water Activities
200-223…**Author's Journal**
224…… Commentary

Alaska *teddy* bear. ☺

ALASKANS

"Gold Fever"

"The Gold Stampede!"

There can be no doubt but that the word "Gold" was the most important word ever uttered in the North Country. It was this word that changed a slow-paced, peaceful and scantily populated land into a hustling, bustling, terror-ridden land where thousands of gold-fevered adventurers arrived daily to play their hand of winner-take-all with the devil, their fellow man and the inhospitable North. The weak, foolish and unadaptable were understandably quickly dealt a losing hand.

Names like Nome, Dead Horse Trail, Klondike, Chilkoot Pass and Skagway, were on the lips of the world. Every story inspired by the gold stampede was stretched and revised twenty-fold from the time of its inspiration to the time when it was put into print by the news-hungry newspapers of America. Stories of the north sold newspapers; the more startling the news the more newspapers were sold. The young and adventurous were helpless against such an onslaught of words, and hoards of them drifted north to pick up the golden nuggets that reportedly "lined every stream and blanketed every hillside".

Still, amidst all this confusion and lawlessness, there roamed a special breed of man who came north to share in its romance and awesome, rugged splendor. They came, not drawn by greed or the promise of instant riches, but by their visions of a new world; a world where a man could be his own man, if he possessed the courage, confidence, faith and natural genius to do so. He was a man who, as Thoreau described such a man, "marched to the beat of his own drums". It is this sort of men, then, that I have tried to portray in much of my artwork. Men, long of years, at peace with themselves and with the world.

Sourdoughs

Mushing

Father Ron Dunfey (traveling priest)

Father Ron Dunfey was a model for many of my "sourdough" paintings. (See Cover).

"The Endless Quest"

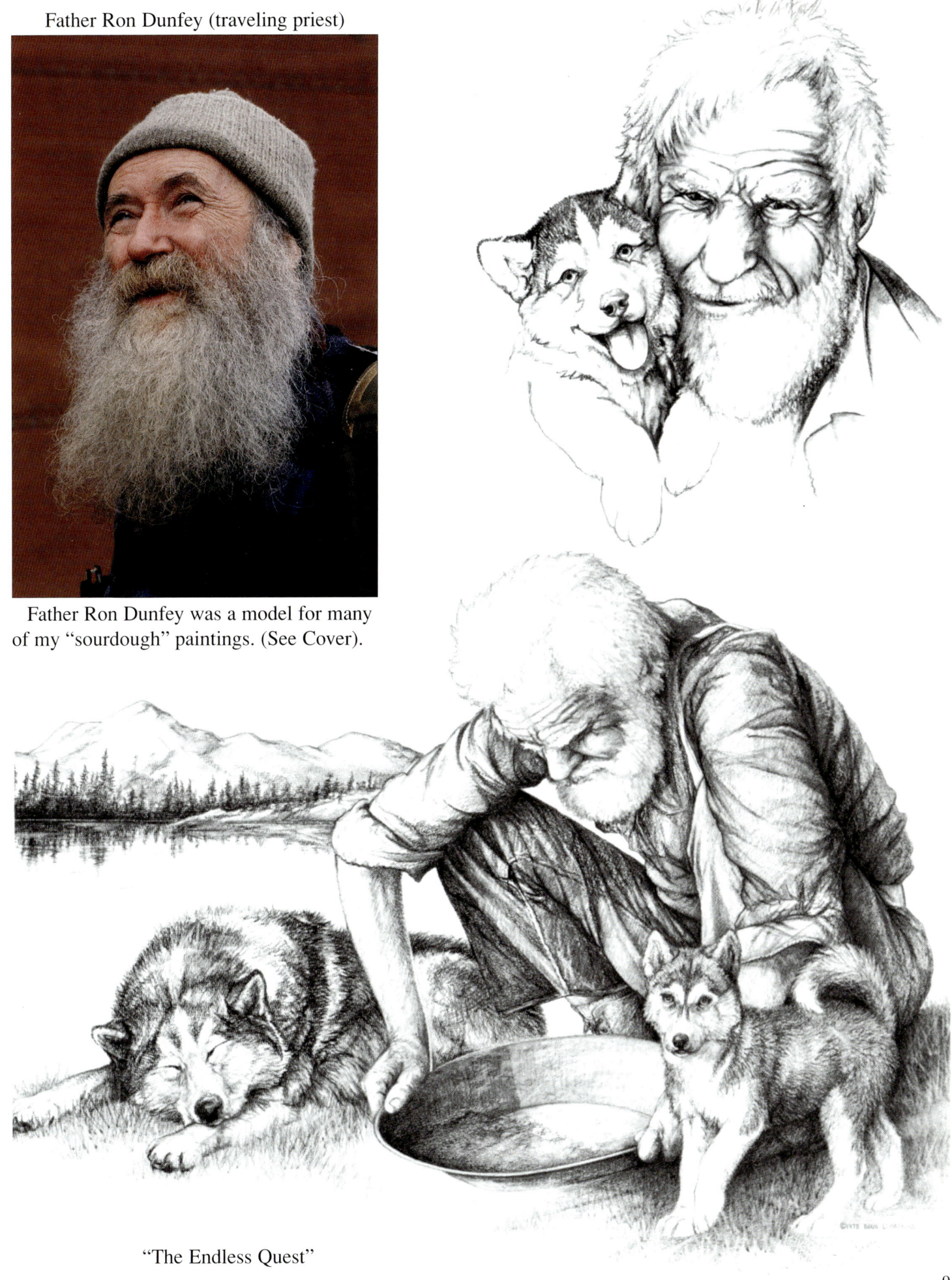

Siberian Husky pups

"Tomcod Fishers"

"Alaska Sunset"

"Pard'ners"

Author's dog "Chinook"

"The Gold Prospector"

Alaska sled dog study

"Breaking Camp"

"The Homestead"

"Happy Trails"

Pups

"Kookena", Alaska Malamute.
**See page 17 to see him all grown up.

Jenny Liska "mushing" my team.

"Cheechako and Sourdough"

Mushing friends Maruska and Jenny.

"Time Out"

Alaska Sled Dogs

Sourdoughs

"Mukluk Warmers"

Alaskan Sled Dogs

"Kookena", Alaska Malamute.
**See page 15 to see him as a pup.

Sluice box

"Smoke n' Snooze"

Sourdoughs

"Armful of Trouble"

"Maybe This Time"

"The Christmas Tree"

"End of the Trail"

"First Snow"

"Mushing Buddies"

"Christmas Mischief"

"Warm n' Cozy"   "Best Friends"

My first four sled dogs (Silver, Shakey, Spooky and Buck).

23

"The Good Life"

Canada geese family / Seward highway / June

"Chinook" (4 years old)

"Citico Charley" was a model for many of my "sourdough" paintings. (See opposite page).

"Chinook" (8 months old) at a remote camp.

"The Alaskan"

Huskies

"The Last Frontier"

Totem pole

"Arctic Handwarmer"

Wood frog. Alaska's only amphibian.

"Here's Trouble"

Mount McKinley, located within Denali National Park and Preserve, is the highest mountain on the North American continent. If measured from the 2,000 foot lowlands to its summit at 20,320 feet, the mountain's vertical relief of about 18,000 feet is greater than that of Mount Everest.

"Hittin' the Trail"

Rich Gorr (Minnesota) watches Charlie Frank (Georgia) pull in another King salmon near Clear Creek. Our guide Rhett prepares to net it.

Katie Decker (Texas) with caribou antlers.

"Proud Alaskan"

29

Emma Kuriscak of Anchorage walks through a field of lupine along Turnagain Arm.

Dall sheep feed on mineral-rich roadside soils near Windy Point (south of Anchorage). This area is a likely place to view sheep; either grazing near the Seward highway or scampering about in the rocky crags above. During tourist-season, "sheep jams" often occur along this narrow stretch of highway.

"Chinook" babysitting injured Hawk Owl at author's winter cabin.

Musher with a very well trained team of dogs.

Joe Liska and his dog Zeke paddle through thin ice on West Lake in mid-November, 2007. The quarter-inch of ice means that it is likely their last trip across the lake and to their cabins until thicker ice forms

Jim Patka with Silver salmon.
Kenai river/October

Mount McKinley and Wonder Lake / Denali National Park

Kyle Draeger holds up a "keeper" King salmon. Gulkana River / 1980's.

A golfer leaves the 9th hole of Moose Run Golf Course, (Anchorage, AK.) in early October. Colorful autumn leaves paint the courses and hillsides "gold" during this season.

Fireweed and Worthington Glacier. Near Valdez / August.

BIRDS OF ALASKA

Tuffed Puffin

the HAWK and EAGLE in Alaska

Alaska Department of Fish and Game
Wildlife Notebook Series

HAWKS AND EAGLES, like owls, are birds of prey but unlike most owls, they are active during the daylight hours. Hawks are often seen perched in trees along the roadside, soaring high overhead or darting rapidly through the woodlands. Like other predators, hawks have been persecuted for many years throughout the United States. However, we are now beginning to understand the true relationships and importance of these very specialized birds to our environment.

GENERAL DESCRIPTION: Most diurnal birds of prey fall into one of three major groups that can be easily identified when the bird is in flight. The *buteos* are soaring hawks with chunky bodies, broad rounded wings, and fan-shaped tails. Buteos found in Alaska are the rough-legged hawk (*Buteo lagopus*), the red-tailed hawk (*Buteo jamaicensis*), the Swainson's hawk (*Buteo swainsoni*), the Harlan's hawk (*Buteo harlani*), the golden eagle (*aquila chrysaetos*) and the bald eagle (*Haliaeetus leucocephalus*). Buteos are summer residents in most of the State, but there is probably a wintering population of red-tailed hawks and both species of eagles in Southern Alaska.

The falcons have streamlined bodies, pointed wings and long narrow tails. Unlike the buteos, falcons fly with short, rapid wing beats and usually do not soar for long periods. Three species nest in Alaska, but migrate south in the fall, and a fourth is a year-round resident. The peregrine falcon, or duck hawk (*Falco peregrinis*); the merlin, or pigeon hawk (*Falco columbarius*); and the kestrel, or sparrow hawk (*Falco sparverius*) are the migratory species. The largest of the falcons, the gyrfalcon (*Falco rusticolus*), is a permanent resident of Alaska's alpine and arctic tundra regions. Peale's falcon, a subspecies of the peregrine, is probably a year-round resident of the Aleutians.

The *accipiters* are woodland hawks characterized by rounded wings and long narrow tails. When hunting, they take "stands" in trees or pursue game by moving through the woodlands with quick wing beats interrupted by short glides. The sharp-shinned hawk (*Accipiter striatus*) is the smallest of this group and is considered a migrant, but some sharp-shins probably winter in Southeastern Alaska. The largest accipiter, the goshawk (*Accipiter gentilis*), is a year-round resident of interior Alaska that is most commonly found in birch and aspen woods throughout the State.

Two other hawks nest in Alaska which are not members of these three groups. They are the harrier, or marsh hawk (*Circus cyaneus*), and the osprey (*Pandion haliaetus*). The marsh hawk is a slim bird with a white patch at the base of the tail, often seen flying low with deliberate wing beats. Its wings form a shallow V when the bird is gliding. The osprey frequents rivers or lakes and flies with a crook in its wings. Ospreys are often observed plunging into water in pursuit of fish.

FOOD HABITS: Buteos subsist on small rodents, and to a lesser extent on hares and grouse. The golden eagle is a powerful hunter that eats hares, grouse, ptarmigan and ground squirrels. The bald eagle lives mainly on fish. Carrion is also important in the diet of most buteos. Peregrine falcons live mainly on waterfowl and other small birds, while the gyrfalcon's diet consists of ptarmigan, ground squirrels and a variety of smaller birds and mammals. Merlins take small birds, and kestrels eat insects, mice and other small rodents. The accipiters hunt grouse, hares and several species of small birds and mammals in dense woodlands. Rodents are the most important food of marsh hawks and ospreys eat fish.

NESTING AND POPULATION: Buteos build large stick nests in trees, old buildings or on cliffs. Accipiters and merlins prefer to build stick nests in trees. A dead snag near water is often selected as a nesting site by ospreys, but they nest on cliffs or even the ground. Peregrines and gyrfalcons select cliffs as nest sites, while tree cavities are often used by kestrels. Ground nests are always used by marsh hawks. Most adult hawks return to the same general nesting area each year, and the same nest is sometimes used for several years. Nests are vigorously defended by adults which employ noisy aerial displays and, occasionally, open attack.

Hawks are predators and do not raise large broods. Many Alaskan hawks have shown a decrease in the production of young in recent years. This is partly due to heavy use of pesticides in wintering areas. Because most prey species (food items) utilized by hawks in wintering areas are contaminated with pesticides, harmful amounts are concentrated in the predator. Many prey species wintering in the south nest in Alaska, and serve as a source of contamination to both migratory and resident hawks. Pesticide residues drastically affect productivity of the hawks by altering reproductive behavior, causing a decrease in eggshell thickness which increases chances for egg breakage, and causing a high proportion of embryos to die before hatching. This situation is cause for serious concern, especially with regard to all migratory birds of prey.

IMPORTANCE: Hawks, like other predators, play an important role is the scheme of nature. They help insure against overpopulation of rodents and other animals. Certain species eat carrion, thus utilizing animals that die from numerous causes. The art of falconry has long been recognized as an effective and exciting method of taking game. Beyond this, for ages people have been fascinated by the grace and power of hawks. There is an unmeasurable value in just seeing a bald eagle soaring high over head or a peregrine falcon making a 100-foot dive at an unwary duck.

MANAGEMENT: It is illegal to kill any bird of prey in Alaska. A permit from the Commissioner of Fish and Game is required to possess a live hawk. Furthermore, the Department of Fish and Game keeps records on nesting areas, and works closely with other land managing agencies to insure protection of critical nesting areas. These precautions are essential so that we can insure perpetuation of these interesting and important birds for future generations.

Jerry D. McGowan

Bald Eagles

A Bald Eagle perches near the Seafarer's Memorial in Homer, Alaska.

Adult   Immature

The Bald Eagle is so named for its conspicuous white head and tail. This distinctive white plumage, however, is not attained until 5 or more years of age. The Bald Eagle has a wing span up to 7 1/2 feet and weighs from 8 to 14 pounds. Like many raptors, males are smaller than females.

Bald Eagles are found only in North America and Alaska has many more eagles than all other states. Alaska's highest nesting densities occur on the islands of Southeast Alaska where the eagles usually nest in old-growth timber along saltwater shorelines and mainland rivers. Further north, the eagles often use old cottonwood trees for their nesting sites.

A bounty was put on eagles by the Alaska Territorial Legislature in 1917. However, in 1953 (after over 100,000 eagles were already killed) the "eagle predation" claim was found to be mainly false and the bounty was removed. It is now illegal to kill or possess any part of any eagle, including feathers.

Bald eagles perch along the Homer Spit in -10 degree January weather. Eagles have been fed during the cold winter months in Homer, Alaska for many years. However, this human feeding will stop in 2010, ending this sometimes controversial practice.

(Author's Journal entry) 26 May, 1975: "20 million shore birds and one million waterfowl are estimated to have moved east through Prince William Sound between April 19 and May 12, 1975. Whenever a Bald eagle would fly over, the whole shoreline of birds would flush."

Adult Bald Eagle

Adult "Golden"

Chick

Talons

Golden Eagles

Alaska Birds of Prey Study

Merlin / Kodiak Island / September

Osprey

Merlin

Sparrow Hawk

42

Sparrow Hawk

Merlin / Denali National Park

Gyrfalcon

Peregrine Falcon

OWLS

Great Horned Owls

Great Horned Owl Chicks

Adult Great Horned Owl

Saw-whet Owl

G. H. Owls

Owls fly almost silently because of the downy edges of their primary wing feathers. And, since they often hunt during the darker hours, their prey is usually unaware that it is under-attack until it is *too late*

Owls are very protective of their nesting site and territories (as is this Great Horned Owl). People and animals that approach too near are often *dive-bombed!*

Great Gray Owls

Owl Chick

Adult Great Gray Owl

Hawk Owls

Bloody-beaked Hawk Owl hunting shrews near Bird Creek, Alaska

Hawk Owl

Owl Study

Screech Owls
Long-Eared Owl
Short-Eared Owl
Saw-whet Owl

Screech Owl

Boreal Owl

Boreal Owl

"Snowy Owls / Fireweed"

Talons

"Snowy Owl / Winter"

Snowy Owl
Attacking Ptarmigan

In the arctic the Snowy Owl hunts ptarmigan, lemmings and other small birds and mammals.

Male Snowy Owls are whiter in color than the more brown-barred females.

Male

Snowy Owl Study

Spruce Grouse
Fanned Tail

Ruffed Grouse

Spruce Grouse

the GROUSE in Alaska

Alaska Department of Fish and Game
Wildlife Notebook Series

BLUE GROUSE (*Dendragapus obscurus*), or "hooters" are restricted to the southeastern part of the state, occurring from Glacier Bay southward, with the exception of Prince of Wales Island.. Dense, coastal forests of tall Sitka spruce and hemlock are the usual haunts of this grouse, but they are often found near timberline among dwarfed alpine firs. Muskeg and alpine meadows are important summer and fall feeding areas for these birds.

The Blue grouse is the largest upland game bird in Alaska with the males sometimes attaining weights of 3 1/2 pounds (1.59 kg). This grouse can be distinguished not only by its large size, but also by the pale band of gray on the tip of its otherwise blackish tail. In spring, the skin on each side of the male's neck develops a deep yellow air sac that becomes encircled with a frill of white feathers when inflated. These air sacs produce the "hoot" of the male, a ventriloquial call sometimes heard over a mile away.

Hens lay 7 to 10 eggs, sometimes as many as 12. The nest is only a depression scratched out in the ground, often located in a grassy opening. As hens begin incubation, the males gather into small flocks. In fall, these flocks disband and the males join the hens and broods. In winter, the birds spend most of their time in coniferous trees where the winter diet of hemlock and spruce needles is obtained.

SPRUCE GROUSE (*Canachites canadensis*), popularly known as spruce hens or spruce chickens, are forest dwellers, and they occur throughout Alaska. They are most common around Bristol Bay, on the Kenai Peninsula, and in wooded valleys along the upper Kuskokwim, Yukon and Tanana rivers. The usual habitat in Alaska is a spruce-birch forest with a lush understory of mountain cranberry, blueberry, crowberry, and spiraea growing on a thick carpet of mosses. The Spruce Grouse of southeastern Alaska differ from the other Alaska spruce grouse. Those in Southeast have white-tipped feathers overlying the base of the tail and do not have a band of rusty brown on the tip of the tail. In Interior and Southcentral Alaska, the brown-tipped tail distinguishes the Spruce Grouse from the Ruffed and Sharp-tailed Grouse.

The cock Spruce Grouse begins courtship displays during the first warm days of April. He struts pompously in a tree or on glistening snow with bright red-eye combs erect, stiffened wings dropped at his sides, tail elevated and fanned, and neck and upper breast feathers ruffed. In May, he also begins to perform peculiar aerial displays by flying steeply downward from a tree and settling to the ground on rapidly beating wings, producing a muffled drumming audible for 100 to 200 yards.

During May, the hen lays 5 to 9 eggs in a shallow nest lined with twigs, leaves, and a few feathers. The nest is usually at the base of a spruce tree but is sometimes beneath a log. The male avoids the hen during incubation and the brooding-rearing period, but he often accompanies the hen and brood in late August. During summer and fall, the birds feed on a variety of flowers, green leaves, and berries, particularly blueberries and mountain cranberries. Insects are an important food for newly hatched chicks. In late August they begin frequenting stream sides, lake shores, and roads in early morning to secure grit for the coming winter months. The sharp, hard particles of rock are apparently essential for grinding the fibrous needles that are the sole source of nourishment in winter. During the short winter days, the birds rest and feed in spruce trees. At night, they either roost on the snow beneath spreading spruce boughs or plummet headlong into the "snow roost," taking advantage of the insulating quality of the dry snow.

RUFFED GROUSE (*Bonasa umbellus*) in Alaska are found in woodlands along the Yukon, Porcupine, Tanana, Kuskokwim, and Upper Copper rivers, and in the Taku and Stikine river drainages in southeastern Alaska. Recently they have been introduced into the Matanuska and Susitna river valleys in southcentral Alaska, where they are flourishing. In summer and fall these birds are often found in alder thickets and alder bottoms, as well as in spruce-birch forests and aspen groves. In winter, aspen-dominated forests are preferred. The species can be recognized by the broad black band near the tip of the tail, the dark colored ruffs on each side of the neck, and the slight crest on top of the head. Two color phases, red and gray, occur.

Males begin the loud "drumming" in April, marking the onset of the breeding season. The cock drums by beating the wings with quick forward and upward strokes while leaning back on the support provided by the fanned tail. The sound is produced by the cupped wings striking the air. Hens lay 6 to 14 eggs in a simple depression in the ground, often located at the base of a tree. Males do not incubate or help rear the young and do not associate with the broods until fall. Probably no other grouse defends its young with such intensity as the Ruffed Grouse hen. If her shrill cry and bold rush in ruffled plumage are not sufficient to ward off a predator, she feigns a broken wing and flutters along the ground in an attempt to distract attention from the concealed chicks.

Principal fall foods include blueberries, highbush cranberries, rose hips, and aspen buds. In winter, the buds and twigs of aspen, willow, and soapberry are major foods.

SHARP-TAILED GROUSE (*Pediocetes phasianellus*) are found in the Yukon River Valley from Canada to Holy Cross, and in the valleys of the Upper Koyukuk, Upper Kuskokwim, Tanana, and Upper Copper rivers. Fire is important in the ecology of the Sharp-tail, since fire maintains the brushy grasslands that are one of the preferred habitats. Other rather open vegetation types are also used, such as spruce bogs, scrubby woodlands, and birch aspen parklands.

Distinctive field marks are the short, pointed tail and the white spots on the wings. The two sexes can be distinguished by close examination of color patterns on feathers of the tail and breast. Courtship displays occur in late April and early May and are performed at dawn on communal dancing grounds called leks. During the displays, cocks produce a hollow booming sound with inflatable air sacs on the neck. The cocks also indulge in much strutting and frenetic dashing about, while the hens wander around the dancing ground with apparent disinterest. Males may mate with several females, and a hen may mate with more than one male. In late May, hens lay 6 to 15 eggs in a shallow nest on the ground, often far from the lek. In early fall, family groups of Sharp-tails gather into flocks. When snow cover persists, the flocks move about a large area. However, males seem to remain quite close to leks in winter. Sharp-tails burrow into snow at night for insulation and concealment. Paper and birch buds and catkins are a staple part of their winter diet. Grass seeds, leaf fragments, insects, aspen buds, and berries are consumed when available.

POPULATION FLUCTUATIONS: Abundance of Alaska game birds varies widely over the years, but rarely are these fluctuations in the classic "10-year cycle." The Blue Grouse of southeastern Alaska and the Spruce Grouse of coastal areas apparently never drop to low levels like the Spruce, Ruffed, and Sharp-tailed Grouse of Interior Alaska. Causes of the fluctuations are not understood, but may involve recurrent changes in climate, food and cover conditions, predator abundance, or genetic makeup of the bird populations. Heavy hunting pressure is never exerted over a large enough area to be responsible for the widespread changes.

HUNTING: Although a large portion of the grouse harvest occurs incidental to other hunting, some specialized methods are used in taking the individual species. One of the more rewarding and sporting means of hunting Blue Grouse is to stalk "hooting" males in April and May. Spruce Grouse hunters generally try to be out on the clear frosty mornings of September and October, when birds are seeking grit at locations where bare soil or gravel is exposed. Ruffed Grouse and Sharp-tails are more difficult to hunt, unless one has a dog. However, these species can sometimes be found "budding" in the tops of aspens and birches in late fall and winter.

Laurence N. Ellison
Revised and reprinted 1994

Range of the Grouse in Alaska (shaded area)

Grouse Study

Spruce Grouse

Spruce Grouse / Autumn

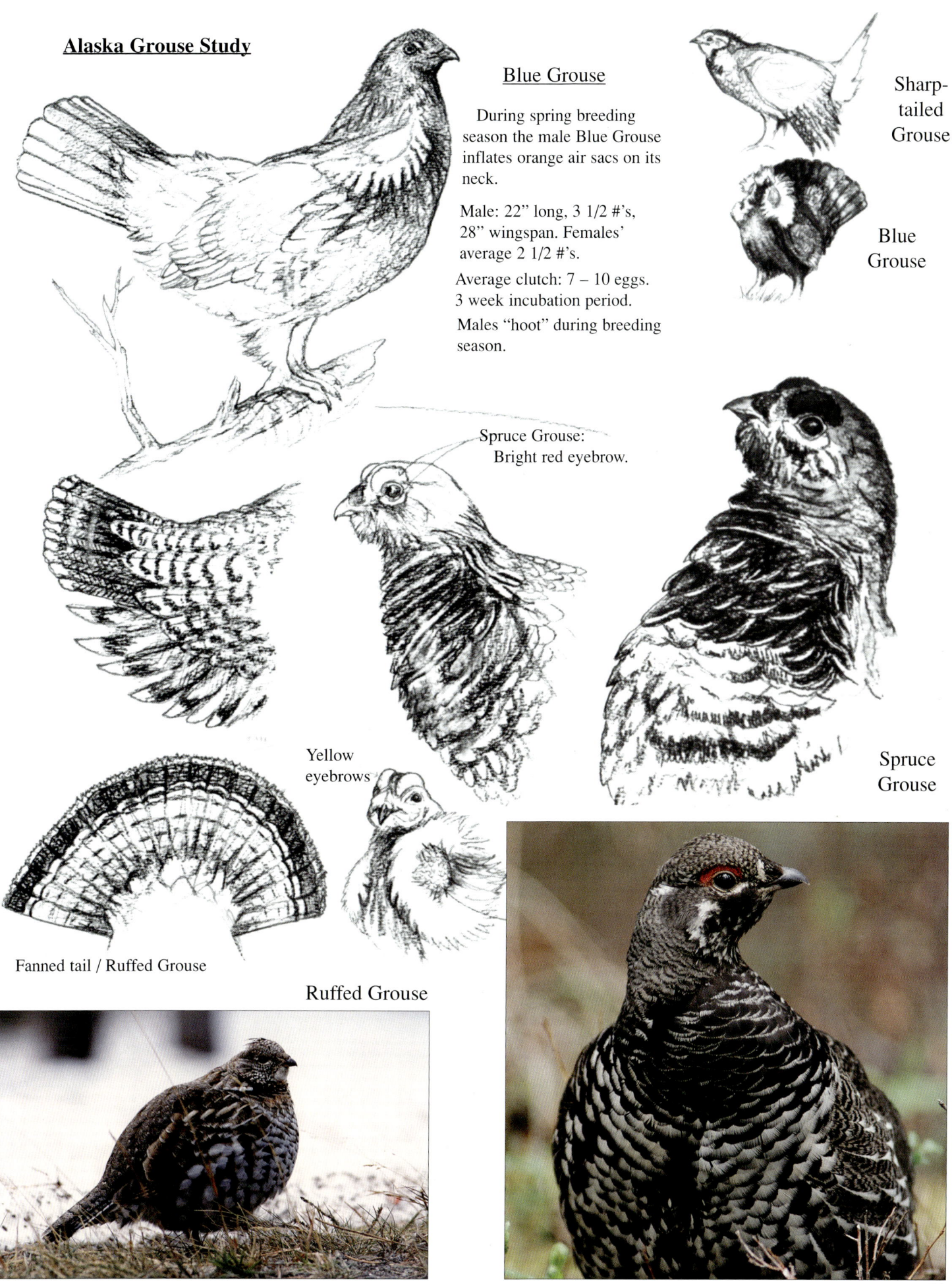

the PTARMIGAN in Alaska

Alaska Department of Fish and Game
Wildlife Notebook Series

Ptarmigan, close relatives of Forest and Prairie Grouse, live in alpine and arctic tundras throughout the northern hemisphere. There are three kinds of ptarmigan, and all are found in Alaska. **WILLOW PTARMIGAN** (*Lagopus lagopus*) are found nearly everywhere in Alaska's high, treeless country. They occupy a broad range throughout Canada, Scandinavia, Finland and Russia. The famous Red Grouse of Scotland is a race of Willow Ptarmigan. **ROCK PTARMIGAN** (*Lagopus mutus*) also live in Canada, Scandinavia, Scotland and northern Eurasia. They range through most of Greenland and Iceland and have scattered southern outposts in Japan, Switzerland, and Spain. In Alaska, Rock Ptarmigan live in all major treeless areas except the flat tundras of the western and northern coasts. **WHITE-TAILED PTARMIGAN** (*Lagopus leucurus*) are strictly North American. They occupy rugged uplands from the Alaska Range and central Yukon southward to Washington and northern New Mexico.

GENERAL DESCRIPTION: Ptarmigan look just like small grouse, weighing from 10 1/2 ounces to 1 1/2 pounds (0.3 - 0.7 kg) except that their toes are feathered, their wings are white all year, and they have pure white body plumage in winter.

LIFE HISTORY: In early spring, male ptarmigan become intolerant of other males and establish territories that they defend vigorously with aerial chases and a variety of gargling, croaking, and screaming noises. Sometimes the three species are found on a single mountain, and often two kinds breed close together. In such cases there is usually a clear altitudinal separation of the various kinds, with Willow Ptarmigan living closest to timberline, Rock Ptarmigan on middle slopes and low ridges, and White-tails high among rough rocky screes and boulder-strewn ridges close to glaciers or snowfields.

All ptarmigan nest on the ground soon after the snow melts. Hens usually lay six to ten eggs which are incubated for three weeks. Hatching takes place in late June and early July throughout Alaska. The male Willow Ptarmigan stays with the family and doesn't hesitate to defend the brood, but male White-tails and Rock Ptarmigan leave the care of chicks entirely to hens. The chicks grow with amazing speed. They can get off the ground only 9 to 10 days after hatching and fly well when they get their first full set of flight feathers at 8 to 10 weeks of age.

Autumn is a time of restlessness. Flocks form and disperse and form again, and the birds move around into unfamiliar alpine areas. In October the wandering takes on a pattern; females tend to form their own flocks and drift lower down into brushy forest openings while cocks stay close to timberline. The extent of the fall movements varies from place to place, but migrations of 100 to 150 miles (160-240 km) one way probably are the longest undertaken by any ptarmigans in Alaska.

Ptarmigan are nomadic in winter, moving erratically from one sheltered slope or patch of food to another from November to March. The birds are quite sociable in winter and usually feed and roost in the snow close together. In April and early May, flocks of ptarmigan numbering several thousand sometimes appear in purposeful movement back to their breeding grounds. These huge flocks, perhaps created by the funneling effect of river valleys and narrow mountain passes, rapidly disintegrate when summering areas are reached, as each cock demands his share of elbow room in the vast stretches of white and brown tundra.

FOODS: When snow covers the ground, Willow Ptarmigan eat willow buds, willow twigs, and a little birch. Rock Ptarmigan nip off birch catkins, birch buds, and a little willow. White-tails mix buds and catkins of willow, birch, and alder in varying amounts. This diet lasts until well along in the courtship period of spring, giving way as snow melts to a blend of insects, overwinter berries, new leaves, and flowers. The birds eat a potpourri of vegetable matter in summer and occasionally take advantage of a particularly abundant crop of caterpillars or beetles. Gradually, as insects disappear and plants become dormant, the diet turns increasingly to berries, seeds, and buds. By mid-October most ptarmigan (except in coastal areas of Southcentral Alaska) are back to their winter menu.

POPULATIONS: Ptarmigan are notorious for their here-today, gone-tomorrow populations, pulsing between superabundance and virtual absence in just a few years. the causes of the rapid population changes remain a mystery. Many people think that the ptarmigan numbers fluctuate rhythmically, with peaks once every 9 or 10 years. Although there is good evidence for these cycles in Iceland, cycles are more legend than proven fact in Alaska. As with many other grouse, the population depends very heavily of each year's production of chicks, since this year's chicks will be next year's breeding stock. Under these conditions, one or two years of poor reproduction or high winter loses can cause drastic declines in abundance. Conversely, one or two good years might result in more ptarmigan than you could shake a shotgun at.

HUNTING: Ptarmigan hunting is fun. You never know what to expect from one trip to the next. On opening day you tramp through colorful thickets of willow and dwarf birch, your dog nosing coveys of brown birds out of the brush while you mop your brow and wish you hadn't put on a sweater. Late in September, after facing a strong, cold wind for several fruitless hours, you top out on a rocky ridge and suddenly find yourself surrounded by several hundred stretch-necked, pinto patterned ptarmigan. You hang up your shotgun for five month, only to be tolled into the hills again by the bright blue days of March. Warmly clad in parka and mukluks, you snowshoe across narrow alpine valleys following meandering trails of three pronged ptarmigan tracks across the brilliant snow.

Ptarmigan hunting can be a serious business, especially if you live in Alaska's vast hinterland and caribou have been scarce. Then is the time to go after ptarmigan in earnest, using all the tricks at your command. Snares are very effective when used by those who know birds well. A favorite method is to build a thin fence of close wet willow branches, leaving small openings where the snares are set. Another technique takes advantage of the fact that ptarmigan drag their feet in soft snow. A series of snare loops are tied into a long line, and the loops are placed flat on the ground around a favorite thicket of willows. Birds step into the loops, drag their feet forward -- and are caught.

Robert B. Weeden
Revised and reprinted 1994

Willow Ptarmigan / June

Ptarmigan Study

Rock Ptarmigan / June

Range of Ptarmigan in Alaska (shaded area)

Top: Willow Ptarmigan (Spring plumage) Bottom: Willow Ptarmigan (Winter plumage)

Willow Ptarmigan (Autumn)

Canada Geese

Range of Canada Geese in Alaska (shaded area)

the CANADA GOOSE in Alaska

Alaska Department of Fish and Game
Wildlife Notebook Series

CANADA GEESE (*Branta canadensis*) are the most familiar geese in Alaska and across North America. They are classified into over 15 subspecies varying in size and shading. All have a distinctive black head and neck with a white cheek patch; most have a full or partial white ring at the base of the neck; brownish wings, back and sides; white to grayish-brown breast and belly; white rump patch; and black legs and feet. Common characteristics of all geese include: similar coloration of males and females; life-long pair bonds with mates (although those that lose mates will re-pair); first breeding at 2-3 years of age; well adapted for walking on land; feed primarily by grazing on vegetation; and they are very social, except during nesting. Pairs generally establish a nesting territory, produce four to five eggs per nest, and raise their young as a family unit. Later, families often combine to form "creches" guarded by several parents. As with most other waterfowl, geese are flightless for about a month in mid-summer, while new wing feathers are grown. Predators of Canada geese and their eggs vary widely among areas and include foxes, coyotes, wolves, bears, wolverines, gulls, eagles, and ravens. Canada geese are popular and accessible to many wildlife watchers, even in urban areas. They are prized by hunters across the continent.

Alaska has six subspecies of Canada geese, two small, two medium, and two large. Cackling Canada geese (*B.c. minima*) are the smallest subspecies, usually weighing 3 to 5 pounds, and they have a distinctive high-pitched call. Cacklers nest only on the outer coast of the Yukon-Kuskokwim Delta in western Alaska and winter primarily in California's Central Valley. In recent years, an increasing number of cacklers has wintered in western Oregon. Spring migration takes cacklers up the Pacific coast, with a stop in Cook Inlet marshes, through the Alaska Range to the nesting grounds. Fall migration includes staging on the upper Alaska Peninsula for several weeks, then a transoceanic flight to Oregon and California. Through the 1970s and early 1980s, overharvest and nest predation reduced the population from over 350,000 to about 30,000. Through a cooperative management effort among wildlife agencies and user groups from Alaska to California, cacklers rebounded to 160,000 by 1993 and are increasing.

ALEUTIAN CANADA GEESE (*B.c. leucopareia*) weigh 4 to 6 pounds and usually have a broader white ring at the base of their necks than other subspecies. These birds are seldom seen in Alaska outside of their Aleutian Islands breeding grounds. They probably follow a coastal migration route through remote areas of the state and across the Gulf of Alaska on their way to and from their wintering grounds in California's Central Valley. A small group of Aleutians nests on the Semidi Islands and winters near Pacific City, Oregon. Although they formerly nested throughout most of the Aleutian Islands, foxes introduced for fur farming between the 1750s and 1939 extirpated Aleutian Canadas from most islands. In 1967, there were fewer than 800 geese in the population and it was listed as an endangered species. An intensive rangewide recovery program and restocking of geese on fox-free islands has ensured their safety. In 1991, the growing population numbered over 7,000 and was downlisted to a threatened species. Most now nest on Buldir Island, with small numbers on Chagulak, Agattu, Nizki, and Kaliktagik islands.

TAVERNER'S (*B.c. taverneri*) and LESSER (*B.c. parvipes*) CANADA GEESE are the two medium-sized subspecies that are very similar and may collectively be called "lessers." They differ only slightly in size and color (*Taverneri* are smaller and darker breasted). These two populations are the most widespread and abundant Canada Goose subspecies in Alaska. Taverner's are geese of coastal tundra, nesting just inland of cackling Canadas on the Yukon-Kuskokwim Delta and extending north to the Arctic Slope. Lesser Canadas (*parvipes*), related to larger subspecies to the east, nest in Cook Inlet and throughout river drainages continuously from western and Interior Alaska to the Yukon Territory. Both subspecies winter primarily in Washington and Oregon. Taverner's Canadas gather at Izembek Lagoon near Cold Bay for a direct trans-Pacific flight. Parvipes take either the Gulf of Alaska coast south or follow interior paths up the Tanana River, through British Columbia.

The DUSKY CANADA GOOSE (*B.c. occidentalis*) is the darkest colored Canada Goose in Alaska. Duskies average 6 to 8 pounds, but males can weigh 10 pounds or more in spring. The population of dusky geese has always been small, with the shortest migration of all Canada geese in Alaska. They nest only on the Copper River Delta near Cordova. Most birds overwinter in the rich grassy fields of Oregon's Willamette Valley and along the Columbia River near Portland, but a few stay farther north in coastal areas of Washington and British Columbia. The great Alaska earthquake of 1964 produced an uplift and drying of their nesting grounds that initially helped duskies increase to over 25,500 by 1979. However, long-term habitat changes favoring predators, such as brown bears and coyotes, have reduced dusky goose production, and the population has hovered between 10,000 and 18,000 since the 1980s.

The largest goose in Alaska, the VANCOUVER CANADA GOOSE (*B.c. fulva*), weighs 6 to 10 pounds during the fall, but males can weigh 12 to 14 pounds in spring. These geese are found in Southeast Alaska and British Columbia where most remain year round. Vancouver geese, unlike other Canadas, nest in coastal forests and winter along marine waters. The biology of these birds is not well known because they are more secretive, frequently building nests and rearing broods in old growth spruce and hemlock forests. Vancouvers sometimes nest in trees. Succulent plants, including skunk cabbage, are favored summer foods, but Vancouvers heavily rely on animal matter during the winter. Clams, salmon eggs, and even dead salmon are readily eaten!

The reader is encouraged to review *Ducks, Geese and Swans of North America* (F.C. Bellrose, 1976, Stackpole Books) and the *Wildlife Notebook Series* entry on Geese.

Text: Tom Rothe
Revised and reprinted 1994

Aleutian Goose

Canada Geese Chicks

Canada Goose Study

A pair of goslings take shelter under their mother's wing.

the GEESE in Alaska

Alaska Department of Fish and Game
Wildlife Notebook Series

In addition to Canada Geese, (see *Wildlife Notebook Series*, "Canada Geese"), four other goose species are commonly found in Alaska: Emperor Goose, Greater White-fronted Goose, Lesser Snow Geese, and Brant.

EMPEROR GEESE (*Chen canagica*) are thought to be the state's most attractive geese. Their throat and lower neck are black, but the remainder of their neck and head are white. The body is bluish-gray with feather edgings of black and white. Emperor Geese have yellow feet and legs and a white tail. They are a medium-sized, but chunky goose, weighing 5 to 7 pounds (2.3-3.2 kg). Their major nesting ground is a small area along the Yukon-Kuskokwim Delta coast, but some nest along coastal areas of northwest Alaska and in Siberia. Emperor Geese lay four to five eggs and are dedicated parents, but first-year survival for the young is relatively low. Nearly all Emperors winter under harsh conditions in the Aleutian Islands, on the western and south side of the Alaska Peninsula, and on Kodiak Island. However, stragglers have occurred as far south as California and even Hawaii! Emperor Geese are sometimes called beach geese. Rarely are they found far from marine water. Although Emperors rely on marsh plants and berries for food during the summer and early fall, in late fall and winter they feed heavily on seaweeds and animal matter, such as clams and snails. The Emperor Goose population declined from an estimated 140,000 in 1964 to 42,000 in 1986. Combined with low first-year survival of young and periods of high nest predation, harvest levels were a contributing factor to the decline. Since 1984, an intensive research and conservation program has promoted an increase to over 71,000 in 1993.

GREATER WHITE-FRONTED GEESE (*Anser albifrons*) are medium-sized, weighing 5 to 7 pounds (2.3-3.2 kg), and are generally grayish-brown on the head, neck, back, and wings. They are distinguishable from other dark geese in Alaska by their pink bills, orange legs (young birds have yellow legs), and three-note laughing call. They were officially named for their white faces, acquired in their first winter, although they are commonly called "specklebellies" for the irregular black bars and spots on the breasts of adults. Immatures are white-breasted or have only small, black feathers.

Three populations of White-fronts breed in Alaska. Pacific Flyway Whitefronts nest mainly on the Yukon-Kuskokwim Delta and Bristol Bay, and winter from central California to Mexico. This population declined from 400,000 to 100,000 birds during the 1970s but grew to over 295,000 by 1993 under restrictive hunting rules. The Tule White-fronted Goose (*A. a. gambelli*), a larger and darker subspecies, numbers only about 7,000 birds and winters with Pacific birds in central California. Its Alaska breeding range has not yet been fully determined, but the west side of Cook Inlet is a known nesting area. White-fronts nesting in the remainder of Alaska (none are found in the Aleutian Islands or Southeast Alaska) are part of the Mid-continent Population that breed throughout the western and central arctic of Canada. This population of over 300,000 birds migrates through the central United States and winters in Texas and Mexico. White-fronts are among the first waterfowl to return in the spring. They nest in a variety of habitats near water, usually some distance from other nesting geese, producing clutches that average four to six eggs. Parents and young form strong family units that remain together until the following breeding season. White-fronts leave Alaska early in fall and most are gone by the third week of September.

BRANT (*Branta bernicla nigricans*) are small (2.5 to 5 pounds or 1.1-2.3 kg) and compact. They are distantly related to Canada Geese. They have a black head and neck, blackish-brown back and wings. dark breast, and white belly. There is a fluted white "necklace" about midneck (except on the young of the year). Young birds have light gray edgings on their wing feathers which are absent on adults. Lighter colored Atlantic Brant are occasionally seen in Alaska during migration. Brant usually travel in wavy lines low to the water and have a guttural, grating call. Brant have been called the "sea goose" because they are never far from salt water year round. Most Pacific Brant nest in colonies along the Yukon-Kuskokwim Delta coast. Scattered nesting also occurs along the northwest coast, arctic slope, and in Siberia, with some moderate-sized colonies in the western Canadian arctic. In the fall, Brant from Alaska, Canada, and Russia spend six to nine weeks on Izembek Lagoon and adjacent areas near Cold Bay. There they feed on eel grass and build up fat reserves for migration. In late October or early November, the brant leave Izembek en masse, in a non-stop migration across the Gulf of Alaska, mostly to Baja Mexico. Smaller numbers winter in British Columbia, Puget Sound, and a few bays along the Oregon and California coasts. A major shift in Brant wintering, from California estuaries to Mexico, occurred by the 1960s. Annually, Pacific Brant numbers are subject to "boom-and-bust" production and have ranged from 110,000 to 185,000 since 1960, with about half coming from Alaska.

LESSER SNOW GEESE (*Chen caerulescens caerulescens*) are medium-sized (4 to 7 pounds or 1.8-3.2 kg) and are completely white except for their black wing tips. Adult birds have pink legs and a pink bill, while the young have grayish-brown bills and legs, and feathers tending to sooty-gray. Dark-bodied "blue phase" Snow Geese, common in the eastern Canadian arctic, have been seen rarely in Alaska. There are very few nesting Snow Geese in Alaska. Most are found on Howe Island, near Prudhoe Bay, in a colony that sprung up in 1971 and has grown to over 450 pairs.

Apparently, they were once numerous on the Seward Peninsula and nested at the mouth of the Yukon River, but climactic conditions or unknown factors led to their disappearance. Most Snow Geese that occur in Alaska are spring and fall migrants, stopping to feed and rest on their routes to and from other nesting grounds. A large portion of the western Canada arctic population, up to 325,000, congregates in the Arctic National Wildlife Refuge in northeastern Alaska during September. These birds breed on Banks Island, Northwest Territory, and feed intensively on the Alaska and Yukon coastal plain before flying through Alberta and Saskatchewan to California for the winter. Snow Geese in western Alaska and those found along the Gulf Coast nest on Wrangel Island in Russia, where the population has ranged from 40,000 to 100,000 birds since 1970. Some of these birds apparently use an over-ocean route in fall from the Alaska Peninsula to California. The remainder take a more leisurely coastal route through Southeast Alaska, stopping at the Stikine River Delta and wintering in Washington and British Columbia. In the spring, on their way north, these birds stop over in Cook Inlet and can often be seen near the mouth of the Kenai River. The timing of ice and snowmelt in spring is more critical on both staging and nesting grounds for Snow Geese than for other geese because they nest in the far north and have a short breeding season. A late spring means that less food may be available on their northern "refueling" areas, and that snow cover may delay or completely prevent nesting. In such years, which may occur frequently at high latitudes, few young Snow Geese will be produced.

Besides these four species and the Canada goose, two other species of geese have been seen in the state. These are the **ROSS' GOOSE** (*Chen rossii*), a small version of a Snow Goose, and the **BEAN GOOSE** (*Anser fabalis*) an Asiatic relative of the Greater White-fronted Goose.

Text: Tom Rothe
Revised and reprinted 1994

Snow Geese

Emperor Goose

69

A pair of banded Snow geese feed in a field outside Wasilla, AK. in mid-April. From here most Snows' fly to Siberia.

Widgeon drake

Widgeon

Mallards

Green-winged Teal

"Mountain Mallards"

©1990 DOUG LINDSTRAND

71

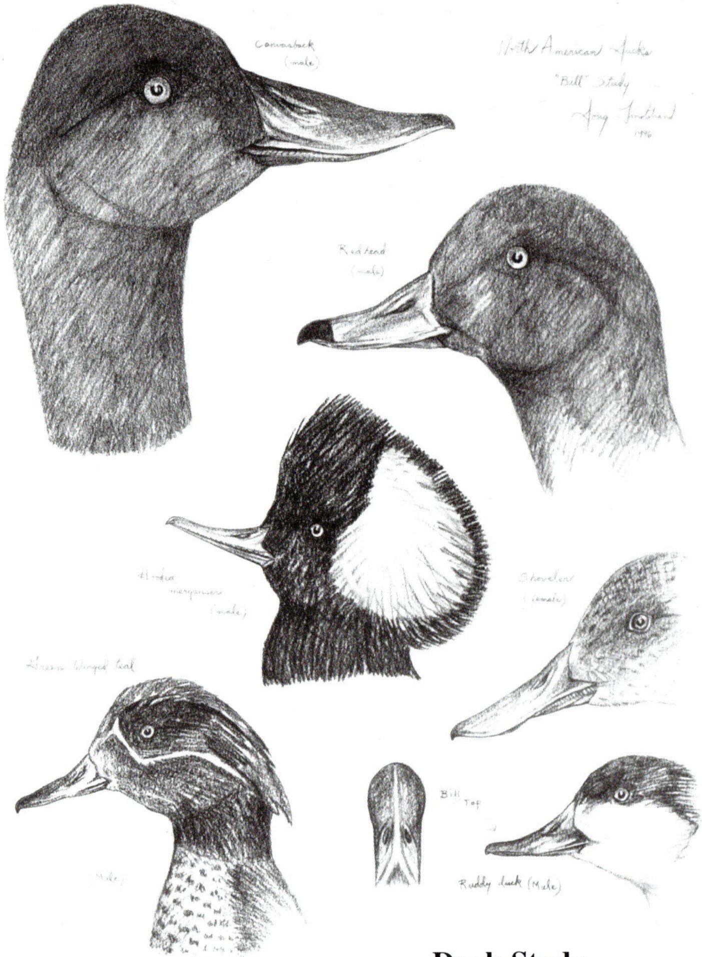

Duck Study    **Mallards**

Hooded Merganser

Mallard
Drake
Study

"Flushed / Mallards"

Mallard hen with ducklings.

73

Mew Gull Chicks

Duck Study

Mallard hen / Fairbanks / springtime

Mallard drake / Fairbanks / springtime

Common Loon / Kenai Peninsula

Mew Gull / Potter Marsh / Anchorage

77

Trumpeter Swans

Whistling Swan

78

Trumpeter swans heading south / October

Juvenile (front) and adult (rear) Trumpeter swans.

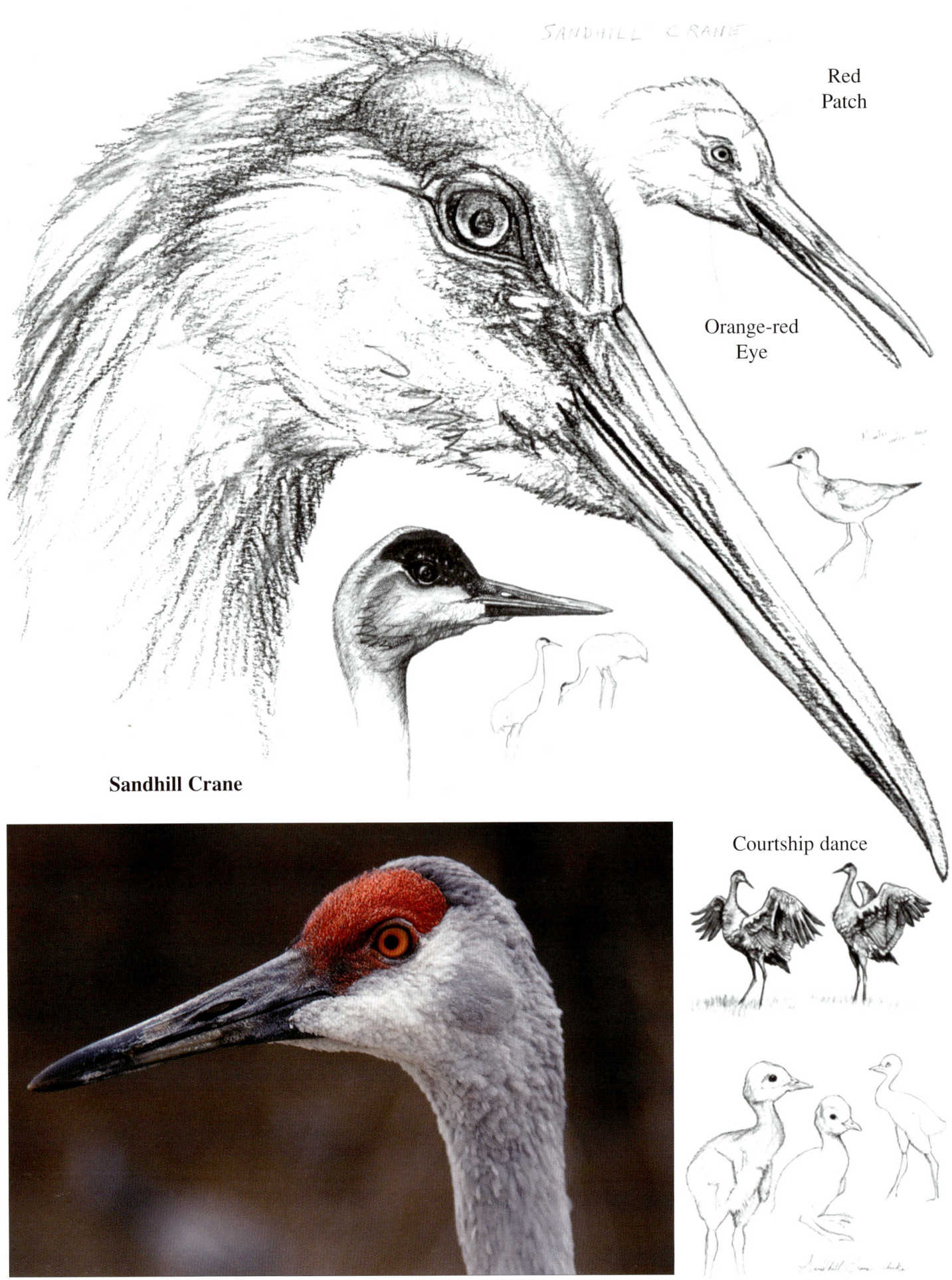

Sandhill Crane Chick

Common Loon / Matanuska Valley

Long-tailed Jaeger hunting rodents.

Ravens flock together during an early November snowstorm near Portage, Alaska.

A Yellowlegs feeds along the shoreline of a saltwater marsh near Anchorage.

Alaska Bird Study

Newly-hatched chicks ride the back of an adult Red-necked Grebe.

Artic terns "hoover" while hunting.

Adult Arctic tern feeding young / June

Gulls fighting above St. Paul Island, Bering Sea

Doug landing row boat at his West Beaver lake cabin. Gull's nest is about 30 yards south.

Killdeer

Common Murres / Pribilof Islands

Tufted Puffins / Resurrection Bay

Horned Puffins

Horned Puffin / Pribilof Islands

Tufted Puffins

Horned Puffins

MAMMALS OF ALASKA

A Brown bear fishes at McNeil Falls / July, 2007

the DALL SHEEP
in Alaska

Alaska Department of Fish and Game
Wildlife Notebook Series

DALL SHEEP (*Ovis dalli dalli*) inhabit the mountain ranges of Alaska. Dall sheep are found in relatively dry country and frequent a special combination of open alpine ridges, meadows, and steep slopes with extremely rugged "escape terrain" in the immediate vicinity. They use the ridges, meadows, and steep slopes for feeding and resting. When danger approaches they flee to the rocks and crags to elude pursuers. They are generally high country animals but sometimes occur in rocky gorges below timberline in Alaska.

Male Dall sheep are called rams. They are distinguished by massive curling horns. The females, called ewes, have shorter, more slender, slightly curved horns. Rams resemble ewes until they are about 3 years old. After that, continued horn growth makes them easily recognizable. Horns grow steadily during spring, summer, and early fall. In late fall or winter horn growth slows and eventually ceases. This is probably a result of changes in body chemistry during the rut, or breeding season. This start-and-stop growth of horns results in a pattern of rings called annuli which are spaced along the length of the horn. These annual rings can be distinguished from the other rough corrugations on the sheep's horns, and age can be accurately determined by counting the annuli. Dall rams as old as 16 years have been killed by hunters, and ewes have been known to reach the age of 19 years. Most generally, a 12-year-old sheep is considered very old. As rams mature, their horns form a circle when seen from the side. Ram horns reach half a circle in about two or three years, three-quarters of a circle in four to five years, and a full circle or "curl" in seven to eight years.

LIFE HISTORY: The young, called lambs, are born in late May or early June. As lambing approaches, ewes seek solitude and protection from predators in the most rugged cliffs available on their spring ranges. Ewes bear a single lamb, and the ewe-lamb pairs remain in the lambing cliffs a few days until the lambs are strong enough to travel. Lambs begin feeding on vegetation within a week after birth and are usually weaned by October. Normally, ewes have their first lamb at age 3 and produce a lamb annually. Sheep have well developed social systems. Adult rams live in bands which seldom associate with ewe groups except during the mating season in late November and early December. The horn clashing for which rams are so well known does not result from fights over possession of ewes, but is a means of establishing order. These clashes occur throughout the year (among females, as well) on an occasional basis. They occur more frequently just before the rut when rams are moving among the ewes and meet unfamiliar rams of similar horn size. Dall rams can sire offspring at 18 months of age, but normally they do not breed successfully until they approach dominance rank (at full curl age and size).

FOOD HABITS: The diets of Dall sheep vary from range to range. During summer, food is abundant, and a wide variety of plants is consumed. Winter diet is much more limited and consists primarily of dry, frozen grass and sedge stems available when snow is blown off the winter ranges. Some populations use significant amounts of lichen and moss during winter. Many Dall sheep populations visit mineral licks during the spring and often travel many miles to eat the soil at these unusual geological formations. As several different bands of sheep meet at mineral licks, ram and ewe groups may mingle and young rams join the ram band which happens to be present at the time. This random contribution of young rams to different ram bands may benefit sheep by maintaining genetic diversity. Sheep are very loyal to their home ranges. Mineral licks are good spots to observe sheep because the animals are so intent on eating the dirt they pay little attention to humans. However, major disturbances such as low-flying aircraft or operating machinery readily drive sheep from the mineral licks.

POPULATIONS: Dall sheep in Alaska are generally in good population health. The remoteness of their habitat and its unsuitability for human use has protected Dall sheep from most problems in the past. However, an increasing human population and more human use of alpine areas may cause future problems for Dall sheep. Mountain sheep in general are extremely susceptible to disease introduced by domestic livestock. If grazing of domestic sheep (or possibly cattle) occurs on their ranges, mass die-offs from disease can be reasonably expected.

Sheep numbers typically fluctuate irregularly in response to a number of environmental factors. Sheep populations tend to increase steadily during long periods of mild weather. Then, sudden population declines may occur as a result of unusually deep snow or other severe winter weather. Low birth rates, predation (primarily by wolves, coyotes, and eagles), and a difficult environment tend to keep Dall sheep population growth rates lower than for many other big game species. However, their adaptation to the alpine environment seems to serve them well. They have survived for thousands of years and are among the more successful animal groups.

HUNTING: Dall sheep produce excellent meat but are relatively small in size (usually less than 300 pounds (136 kg) for rams and 150 pounds (68.1 kg) for ewes), and it is difficult to retrieve meat from the rugged alpine areas which they inhabit. These factors have limited sheep hunting to a relatively few, hardy individuals whose interest is more in the challenge and satisfaction of mountain hunting and the alpine experience than in getting food. Recreational hunting is limited to the taking of mature rams during August and September. Many recreational hunters are very selective and choose not to kill a ram unless it is unusually attractive. Instead, these hunters often choose to watch sheep and share their environment.

In some communities of the Brooks Range, Dall sheep are hunted for subsistence. These hunts commonly take place during winter when snow machine travel makes it easier to reach the sheep and retrieve the meat. Subsistence regulations commonly allow taking of all sex and age classes of sheep. Populations which support subsistence hunting must be closely watched to assure that populations are not overexploited.

Photography of Dall sheep is popular for many visitors and residents of Alaska and is not limited by season.

Text: Wayne E. Heimer
Revised by Ken Whitten and reprinted 1994

**"This information was excerpted from the Alaska Department of Fish and Game's Wildlife Notebook Series. For a copy of the complete series, call 907-465-4190 or write ADF&G, Division of Wildlife, P.O. Box 25526, Juneau, Alaska 99811".

Dall sheep in Denali National Park

Author with Dall rams.

Dall Ram

Dall Ram

Dall ewe and lamb / June

Lambs at play. Chugach Mountains

Sheep Study

"Dall Ram / Alaska Range"

Dall lambs stop to look at perhaps the first person they have ever seen.

Ram Study

A full-curl Dall ram browses on rose hips in the Chugach Mountain

96

OLD ONE EYE

Old One Eye was a ram who lived his life in the Chugach Mountains south of Anchorage, Alaska until he ventured too near the Seward highway on November 19, 2003 and was shot and left at the roadside. When he tumbled down the mountain he broke off his right horn, a horn that was likely over 40" in length. The meat was recovered by a local charity and the horns will be kept by the Alaska Department of Fish and Game. There is, as of this November date, a reward of over $3,000 for information leading to the conviction of the person responsible for this senseless criminal act.

Old One Eye was a ram that this book's author knew well and had sketched and photographed over many years. He was one of the area's most dominant rams, even though he lost his right eye during a fight with another large ram during the autumn rut of 1999. He survived Alaska's severe winters, dangerous terrain, and predators, but he could not survive a gunshot as he battled other rams for breeding rights in the closed hunting area of Chugach State Park. He was 11 or 12 years old and was a superb specimen. I will surely miss him, as I had spent many hours with him over the years in the mountains so near by Alaska home.

"Old One Eye" feeding in January, 2003. Chugach Mountains, Alaska.

Ewe with lamb

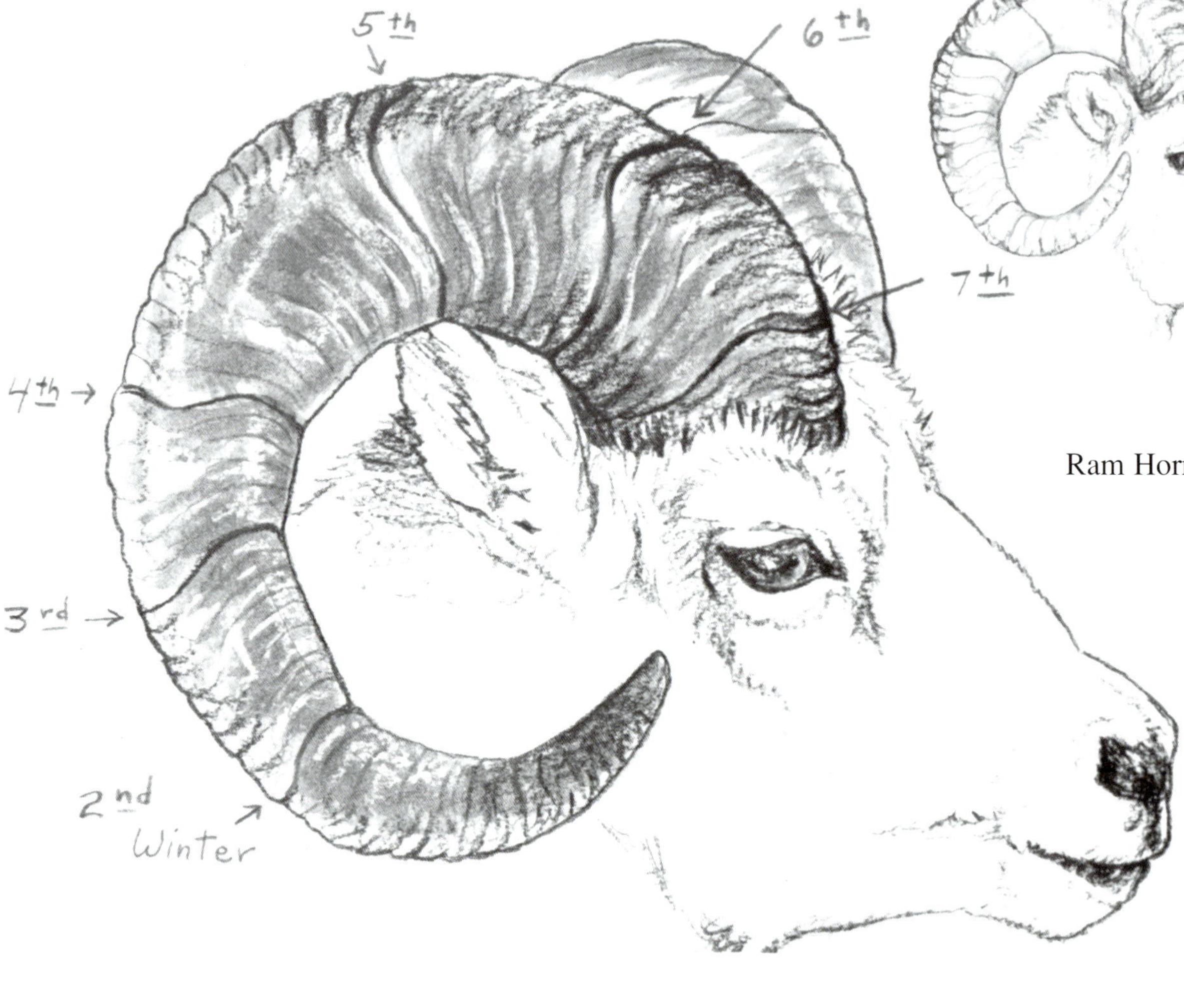

5th
6th
4th
7th
3rd
2nd Winter

Ram Horn Study

Dall Sheep Study

Dall Rams / Chugach Range

The Decker family of Texas pauses to watch a small band of Dall sheep in Denali National Park.

8# lambs are born during May/June and are very vulnerable to predators during the first few days of their lives.

TRACKS

101

Dall Sheep

the MOOSE in Alaska

Alaska Department of Fish and Game
Wildlife Notebook Series

MOOSE *(Alces alces)* are the world's largest members of the deer family. The Alaska race *(Alces alces gigas)* is the largest of all the moose. Moose are generally associated with northern forests in North America, Europe, and Russia. In Europe they are called "elk. " In Alaska, they occur in suitable habitat from the Stikine River in the Panhandle to the Colville River on the Arctic Slope. They are most abundant in recently burned areas that contain willow and birch shrubs, on timberline plateaus, and along the major rivers of Southcentral and Interior Alaska.

GENERAL DESCRIPTION: Moose are long-legged and heavy- bodied with a drooping nose, a "bell" or dewlap under the chin, and a small tail. Their color ranges from golden brown to almost black, depending upon the season and the age of the animal. The hair of newborn calves is generally red-brown, fading to a lighter rust color within a few weeks. Newborn calves weigh 28 to 35 pounds (13-16 kg) and within five months grow to over 300 pounds (136 kg). Males in prime condition weigh from 1,200 to 1,600 pounds (542-725 kg). Adult females weigh 800 to 1,300 pounds (364-591 kg). Only the bulls have antlers. The largest moose antlers in North America come from Alaska, the Yukon Territory, and the Northwest Territories of Canada. Trophy class bulls are found throughout Alaska, but the largest come from the western portion of the state. Moose occasionally produce trophy-size antlers when they are 6 or 7 years old, with the largest antlers grown at approximately 10 to 12 years of age. In the wild, moose rarely live more than 16 years.

LIFE HISTORY: Cow moose generally breed at 28 months, though some may breed as young as 16 months. Calves are born any time from mid-May to early June after a gestation period of about 230 days. Cows give birth to twins 15 to 75 percent of the time, and triplets may occur once in every 1,000 births. The incidence of twinning is directly related to range conditions. A cow moose defends her newborn calf vigorously. Calves begin taking solid food a few days after birth. They are weaned in the fall at the time the mother is breeding again. The maternal bond is generally maintained until calves are 12 months old at which time the mother aggressively chases her offspring from the immediate area just before she gives birth.

Moose breed in the fall with the peak of the "rut" activities coming in late September and early October. Adult males joust during the rut by bringing their antlers together and pushing. Serious battles are rare. Bulls may receive a few punctures or other damage and occasionally die from their wounds. The winner usually mates with the female.

By late October, adult males have exhausted their summer accumulation of fat and their desire for female company. Once again they begin feeding. Antlers are shed as early as November, but mostly in December and January.

FOOD HABITS: During fall and winter, moose consume large quantities of willow, birch, and aspen twigs. In some areas, moose actually establish a "hedge" or browse line 6 to 8 feet above the ground by clipping most of the terminal shoots of favored food species. Spring is the time of grazing as well as browsing. Moose eat a variety of foods, particularly sedges, equisetum (horsetail), pond weeds, and grasses. During summer, moose feed on vegetation in shallow ponds, forbs, and the leaves of birch, willow, and aspen .

MOVEMENTS: Most moose make seasonal movements to calving, rutting, and wintering areas. They travel anywhere from only a few miles to as many as 60 miles during these transitions.

POPULATION DYNAMICS: Moose have a high reproductive potential and can quickly fill a range to capacity if not limited by predation, hunting, and severe weather. Deep crusted snow can lead to malnutrition and subsequent death of hundreds of moose and decrease the survival of the succeeding year's calves.

Moose are killed by wolves and black and brown bears. Black bears take moose calves in May and June. Brown bears kill calves and adults the entire time the bears are out of their winter dens. Wolves kill moose throughout the year. Predation limits the growth of many moose populations in Alaska.

HUNTING: More people hunt moose than any other of Alaska's big game species.

ECONOMIC AND FUTURE STATUS: Because moose range over so much of Alaska, they have played an important role in the development of the state. At one time professional hunters supplied moose meat to mining camps. Historically, moose were an important source of food, clothing, and implements to Athapaskan Indians dwelling along the major rivers. Today, Alaskans and nonresidents annually harvest approximately 6,000 to 8,000 moose— some 3.5 million pounds of meat. Moose are an important part of the Alaska landscape, and tourists photograph those animals that feed along the highway.

Man's developments in Alaska include many alterations upon the face of the land. These activities create conflicts between man and moose as moose eat crops, stand on airfields, eat young trees, wander the city streets, and collide with cars and trains.

Man's removal of mature timber through logging and careless use of fire has, in general, benefited moose as new stands of young timber have created vast areas of high-quality moose food. The future for moose is reasonably bright because man is learning how to manipulate habitat with wildfire and is becoming more skilled at managing factors that limit moose populations, such as predation and hunting.

Text: Robert A. Rausch and Bill Gasaway
Revised by Charles C. Schwartz and reprinted 1994

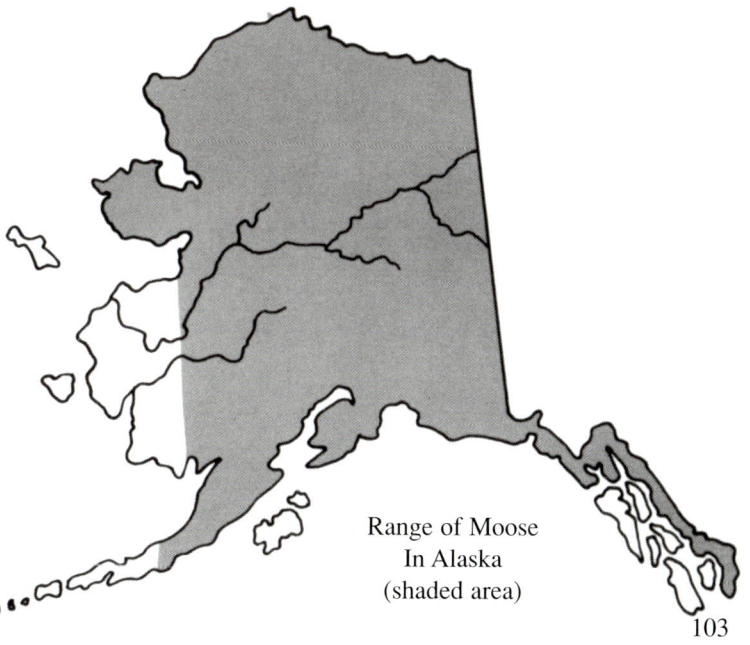

Range of Moose
In Alaska
(shaded area)

Denali

Wolf Pack

August

"Bull Moose / Denali"

Moose calf / June

Bull moose shedding "velvet" in early September.

Cow and bull moose. Mid-September / Interior Alaska

"Survival of the Fittest"

Alaska's large predators often compete for prey and food. This painting depicts a wolf and grizzly competing for a dead moose. Perhaps a wolf pack killed the moose and the grizzly drove them away? Or perhaps the moose died from injuries suffered during the battles of the autumn "rut" and the two predators are jousting for feeding rights? "Survival of the Fittest" is truly a fact of life here in the wilds of Alaska.

White Moose

Moose calves

A cow moose and calves feed on the brush in the McHugh Creek area south of Anchorage. A run-in between the cow and a porcupine resulted in the "porkie" *losing* the ensuing fight. Note the *quills* in the cow's front leg.

The antlers of a bull moose, shed yearly, can spread 80" wide and weigh over 60 pounds.

the CARIBOU in Alaska

Alaska Department of Fish and Game
Wildlife Notebook Series

CARIBOU (*Rangifer tarandus*) are generally associated with the arctic tundra, mountain tundra and northern forests of North America, Russia, and Scandinavia. This species has been a distinctive part of the Alaska fauna for thousands of years and occurs throughout the state except for the southeastern Panhandle and most offshore islands.

In Europe, caribou are called reindeer, but in Alaska and Canada only the domestic forms are called reindeer. All caribou and reindeer throughout the world are considered to be the same species. Alaska has only the barrenground subspecies, but in Canada the barren-ground, woodland, and Peary subspecies are found. The barren ground caribou generally inhabits arctic tundra and open tundra lands near or above timberline, but they may also use large forest habitats during winter.

GENERAL DESCRIPTION: Caribou are large, rather stout members of the deer family with large, concave hoofs that spread widely to support the animal in snow and soft tundra. The feet also function as paddles when it swims.

Caribou are the only member of the deer family in which both sexes grow antlers. Antlers of adult bulls are large and massive; those of adult cows are much shorter and are usually more slender and irregular. In late fall, caribou are clove-brown with a white neck, rump, and feet and often have a white flank stripe. The hair of newborn calves is generally reddish-brown but may range from pale beige to dark brown. Newborn calves weigh an average of 13 pounds (5.9 kg) and may double their weight in 10-15 days. Weight of adult bulls averages 350-400 pounds (159-181.8 kg). However, weights of 700 pounds (318 kg) have been recorded in the Aleutian Islands. Mature females average 175-225 pounds (79.5-120.3 kg). Caribou in northern Alaska are generally smaller than caribou in the Interior and in southern parts of the state.

LIFE HISTORY: After a summer of grazing on succulent vegetation, caribou enter the fall in prime condition. Mature bulls frequently have more than three inches of fat on the back and rump. The shedding of velvet in late August and early September by large bulls marks the approach of the rutting (breeding) season. The bulls cease feeding and show increasing aggressiveness that soon results in combat. Most fights between bulls are brief bouts, but fights occasionally become violent and injuries are not uncommon. Most females do not breed until their third fall. By late October, adult males have exhausted their summer accumulation of fat and once again begin feeding. The largest bulls shed their antlers immediately after the rut and most adult males are "bald" by January. Young animals and non-pregnant cows retain their antlers until April or early May. Pregnant females usually retain their antlers until calves are born in late May or early June.

As the spring migration begins, females and many calves of the previous year congregate as they move to the calving area. In late May or early June a single calf is born (twins are very rare). Newborn calves can walk within an hour of birth. After a few days, they can outrun a man and swim across lakes and rivers.

FOOD HABITS: Like most herd animals, the caribou must keep moving to find adequate food. This distributes feeding pressure and tends to prevent overgrazing. Caribou are great wanderers and very efficient at moving across both boggy and rugged terrain. They commonly travel vast distances to reach suitable foraging sites on widely separated season ranges. In summer, caribou eat a wide variety of plants, apparently favoring the leaves of willows, grasses, and herbaceous and flowering plants. They switch to lichens, "reindeer moss," and dried sedges during winter.

MOVEMENTS: The Alaska caribou is largely a foothills and mountains animal, associated with areas altitudinally or latitudinally above or near timberline, but its movements are extensive and intermittently unpredictable. Calving areas tend to be traditional, but wintering areas used for many years may suddenly be abandoned as the herd changes its migration. This can create problems for the Native people in Alaska and Canada who depend upon caribou for food.

Annual caribou migrations are directional, long-distance treks occurring in spring and early fall. Adult cows and young females move to traditional calving grounds and then to summering areas. The bulls follow far to the rear and scatter widely during the summer. In midsummer, caribou are often harassed by hordes of mosquitos, warble flies, and nose flies. Sometimes the animals will run in a frenzy for long distances, stopping to rest only when exhausted or when wind offers relief from the insects. In the fall and early winter, the herd assembles for the rut and then moves to wintering grounds.

HUNTING: The adult bull caribou is one of the most unique and impressive trophy animals in the North. Each year several thousand nonresident hunters travel to Alaska in search of these nomads. However, the caribou's greatest consumptive value has been as a food animal for Alaska's residents, and thousands are harvested each year. For many Native Alaskans, the caribou is still a major source of food. Alaska's great caribou herds have become increasingly treasured as a natural wonder of state, national, and international importance.

POPULATION DYNAMICS: Approximately 900,000 wild caribou exist in Alaska in about 25 more or less distinct herds. A herd is a group of caribou which establishes a calving area distinct from any other group and calves there repeatedly. The size and distribution of both individual herds and the statewide population have fluctuated in the past, and undoubtedly will in the future. These fluctuations have caused people to believe that caribou are less manageable than other big game species. Also, labeling caribou as wilderness animals has caused people to believe that the decline of caribou is inevitable as civilization encroaches upon the wilderness. However, recent research has shown that caribou are as manageable and adaptable as many other big game species. Caribou can coexist if man will let them. The challenge is for man to give adequate consideration so the great caribou herds will always remain.

Text: James E. Hemming
Revised and reprinted 1994

Spooked

Range of the
Barren Ground Caribou
(shaded area)

(in "velvet")

Caribou in moonlight / Mt. McKinley

"Autumn Caribou / Denali"

Caribou Study / April - October

Bull / "velvet" just shed.

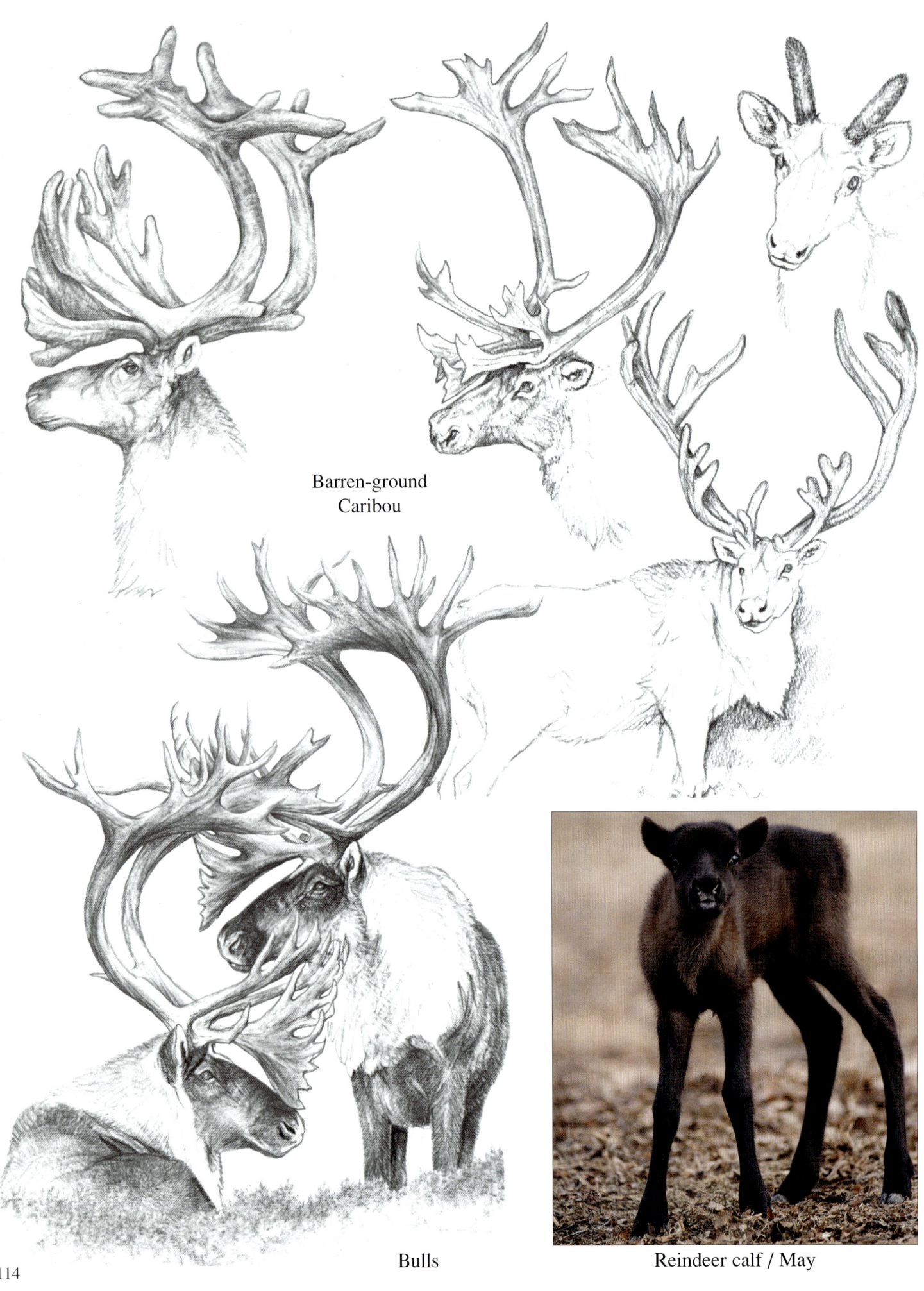

Barren-ground Caribou

Bulls

Reindeer calf / May

Caribou Study

Bull Caribou / September

Bull Caribou / summer. A shuttle-bus follows the bull down the Denali Park road.

Wolves are carnivores, and caribou and moose are their primary food in most of mainland Alaska. In Southeast Alaska, Sitka black-tailed deer are a common prey. And, although wolves most often hunt these large mammals in family packs, "loners" like this wolf (that this book's author followed off-and-on for two days) usually hunt small game and bypass the more dangerous large mammals.

A Bull who has recently shed his antler's "velvet".

A barren-ground Caribou bull (with antlers still in "velvet") roams through the September "colors" in Denali National Park. Caribou are the most migratory of all North American mammals and the herds often roam outside the boundaries of the National Park and are then subject to hunting.

Caribou bull / Denali / August

Caribou bulls / July

Field-Sketches

Field-sketching is a method of capturing an idea, pose, or the "essence" of something in nature. Usually I don't do a whole lot of detail work outside; preferring my studio for that. Also, nowadays I often photograph while sketching landscapes and animals and these photographs plus my sketches will usually provide me with all my needed reference material.

"Autumn Splendor"

This charcoal and watercolor painting was based on some field-sketching doodles (including those shown above) that I did while following a small batch of Caribou bulls for an afternoon. Animals in National Parks are often used to seeing people and hence are much easier to approach.

I flew these Ultra-lights for a few years in the early '80's. My *brilliant* idea was to scout new areas, spot animals and then fly over them and take pictures. Yah, Right! Truth is, I was too busy trying to keep this "kite" stable and upright, then to *even think* about trying to focus a camera! But, it was exciting and I saw some new country.

On a sad note, my initial instructor (Mike J.) was killed in an Ultra-light accident some years later.

the BROWN BEAR in Alaska

Alaska Department of Fish and Game
Wildlife Notebook Series

BROWN BEARS (*Ursus arctos*) occur throughout Alaska except on the islands south of Frederick Sound in southeastern Alaska, the islands west of Unimak in the Aleutian Chain, and the islands of the Bering Sea. They also occur in Canada, Asia, Europe, and in limited numbers in a few western states. Brown bears are very much a part of the Alaska scene and are a favorite topic with most hunters, hikers, photographers, and fishers.

GENERAL DESCRIPTION: Formerly, taxonomists listed brown and grizzly bears as separate species. Technically, brown and grizzly bears are classified as the same species, *Ursus arctos*. Brown bears on Kodiak Island are classified as a distinct subspecies from those on the mainland because they are genetically and physically isolated. The shape of their skulls also differs slightly.

The term "brown bear" is commonly used to refer to the members of this species found in coastal areas where salmon is the primary food source. Brown bears found inland and in northern habitats are often called "grizzlies." In this paper, brown bear is used to refer to all members of *Ursus arctos*.

The brown bear resembles its close relative the black bear, *Ursus americanus*. The brown bear, however, is usually larger, has a more prominent shoulder hump, less prominent ears, and longer, straighter claws. Both the prominent hump and the long claws of the brown bear are adaptations that are related to feeding behavior. The long claws are useful in digging for roots or excavating burrows of small mammals. The musculature and bone structure of the hump are adaptations for digging and for attaining bursts of speed necessary for capture of moose or caribou for food. Color is not a reliable key in differentiating these bears because both species have many color phases. Black bears, for example, occur in many hues of brown, and even shades of blue and white. Brown bear colors range from dark brown through light blond.

Bear weights vary depending on the time of year. Bears weigh the least in the spring or early summer. They gain weight rapidly during late summer and fall and are waddling fat just prior to denning. At this time most mature males weigh between 500 and 900 pounds (180-410 kg) with extremely large individuals weighing as much as 1,400 pounds (640 kg). Females weigh half to three-quarters as much. An extremely large brown bear may have a skull 18 inches long (46 cm) and 12 inches wide (30 cm). Such a bear, when standing on its hind feet, is about 9 feet (2.7 m) tall. Inland bears are usually smaller than coastal bears, probably because they do not have a readily available supply of protein-rich food, such as salmon, in their diet.

Brown bears have been known to live 34 years in the wild, though this is rare. Usually, old males may reach 22 years. Old females may live to 26. Brown bears have an especially good sense of smell and under the right conditions may be able to detect odors more than a mile distant. Their hearing and eyesight are probably equivalent to that of humans. When bears stand upright, it is not to get ready to charge but to test the wind and to see better.

LIFE HISTORY: Mating takes place from May through July with the peak of activity in early June. Brown bears generally do not have strong mating ties. Individual bears are rarely seen with a mate for more than a week. Males may mate with more than one female during breeding season. The hairless young, weighing less than a pound, are born the following January or February in a winter den. Litter size ranges from one to four cubs, but two is most common. Offspring typically separate from their mothers as 2-year olds in May or June. Following separation, the mother can breed again and produce a new litter of cubs the following year. In some parts of Alaska, research results reveal that offspring may not separate from their mothers until they are 3 to 5 years old. This appears to be most common in areas where food is scarce. In some of these areas, females may skip one to three years before producing new litters.

Bear populations vary depending on the productivity of the environment. In areas of low productivity, such as on Alaska's North Slope, studies have revealed bear densities as low as one bear per 300 square miles. In areas teeming with easily available food, such as Admiralty Island in Southeast Alaska, densities as high as one bear per square mile have been found. In central Alaska, both north and south of the Alaska Range, bear densities tend to be intermediate, about one bear per 15-23 square miles. These are average figures which shouldn't be interpreted to mean that each bear has this much territory for its exclusive use. The area occupied by any individual bear may overlap that used by many other individuals.

SAFETY: All brown bears should be treated with respect and can be safely observed only from a distance of at least 100 yards. This is especially true for family groups of a female and her offspring as mother bears are very protective towards their young. Bears protecting a food source, such as the buried carcass of a moose or caribou, should also be treated with special caution. In bear country, campers can best avoid conflicts with bears if they minimize food odors, store their food out of a bear's reach and away from their camp, and avoid camping on bear travel routes.

FOOD HABITS: Like humans, brown bears consume a wide variety of foods. Common foods include berries, grasses, sedges, horsetails, cow parsnips, fish, ground squirrels, and roots of many kinds of plants. In some parts of Alaska, brown bears have been shown to be capable predators of newborn moose and caribou. They can also kill and consume healthy adults of these species and domestic animals. Bears are fond of all types of carrion as well as garbage in human dumps.

Except for females with offspring and breeding animals, bears are typically solitary creatures and avoid the company of other bears. Exceptions to this occur where food sources are concentrated such as streams where bears can catch salmon swimming upstream to spawn. At McNeil River Falls, the largest concentration of brown bears occurs annually. Biologists have observed more than 60 bears at one time, attracted by spawning salmon.

WINTER DORMANCY: In the winter when food is unavailable or scarce, most Alaska brown bears enter dens and hibernate through the winter. While in this state, their body temperatures, heart rate, and other metabolic rates are reduced. Their need for food and water is eliminated. In northern areas with long hard winters, bears may spend from 5 to 7 1/2 months in dens. In areas with relatively warmer winters, such as Kodiak Island, a few bears may stay active all winter. Pregnant females are usually the first to enter dens in the fall. These females, with their newborn cubs, are the last to exit dens. Adult males, on the other hand, appear to enter dens later and emerge earlier than most other bears.

HUNTING: Bear hunting is popular in Alaska and, with proper management, can occur without causing populations to decline. Bear hunting seasons are held in both spring and fall in some areas but only in fall in other areas. Cubs and females with offspring may not be killed. Bear meat should be thoroughly cooked to prevent contracting trichinosis, a parasitic disease which may be fatal to man.

Hunters should examine bears closely with binoculars before shooting to determine if the pelt has spots where the hair has been rubbed away. Such rubbed spots result in a poorer quality hide. A little extra time spent observing a bear before shooting may also prevent the hunter from taking a female that has cubs hidden nearby. An excellent guide to judging trophy brown bears and distinguishing between sexes of bears is the "Take a Closer Look" video which is available for viewing at most Alaska Department of Fish and Game offices.

RESEARCH AND CONSERVATION: Because Alaska contains over 98 percent of the United States population of brown bears, and more than 70 percent of the North American population, it has a special responsibility for this large carnivore. The Alaska Department of Fish and Game is responsible for managing bears in Alaska and for ensuring that management is based on scientific knowledge of the biology of bear populations. Important components of this management effort include maintaining healthy populations of bears throughout Alaska, preservation of bear habitat, prevention of overharvest, and conducting the studies necessary to understand population requirements. As Alaska continues to develop, it is increasingly important for the public to recognize that maintaining sufficient amounts of habitat for brown bears to continue to thrive in Alaska will mean forgoing opportunities for some kinds of economic development in some places.

Text: Sterling Eide and Sterling Miller
Revised by Harry Reynold and reprinted in 1994

Brown bear
Study

A Brown bear sow gives a cub a piggyback ride through a field of sedge grass in the McNeil River area. At times, both of her young cubs managed to crawl atop her as she fed on the grass.

Range of Brown Bear in Alaska (shaded area)

Normally, heavy snowfall in late autumn will drive bears into their winter dens.

Grizzly / Brown bear

124

Grizzly / Brown bear

Brown bear
Study

"Here's Looking At You"

Formerly, taxonomists listed Brown and Grizzly bears as separate species. Technically, however, Brown and Grizzly bears are the same specie, *Ursus arctos*. However, the Brown bears of Kodiak are classified as a distinct sub-specie because they are physically and genetically *isolated*.

A Brown bear captures a chum salmon at McNeil Falls in early July. This book's author was there from July 4th to 8th (2007) and the chum salmon had not yet *peaked* in the area's streams. At the "Falls" the best fishing areas were staked out by the larger and most aggressive males, leaving the less productive sites to the other bears.

"Triple Trouble"

Bears will often *bluff-charge* people, other bears, and other animals to protect their food, cubs, or their *space*. Of course, not all charges are bluff-charges and so intruding *near* a bear can be *extremely dangerous*.

When food is plentiful, both young and adult bears engage in playful fighting.

Grizzly Study

Grizzly paws and claws.

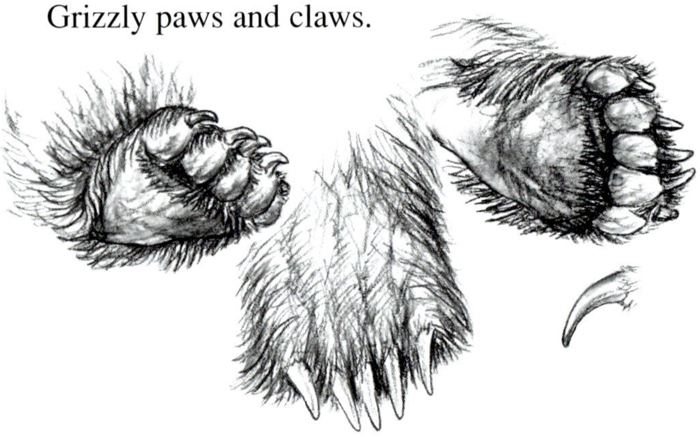

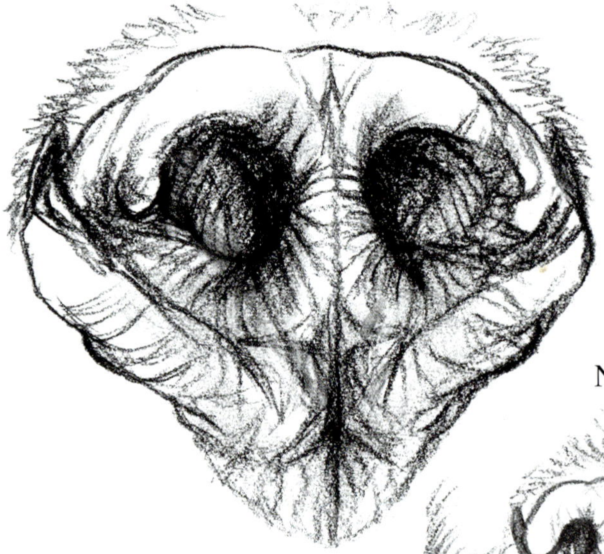

Nose

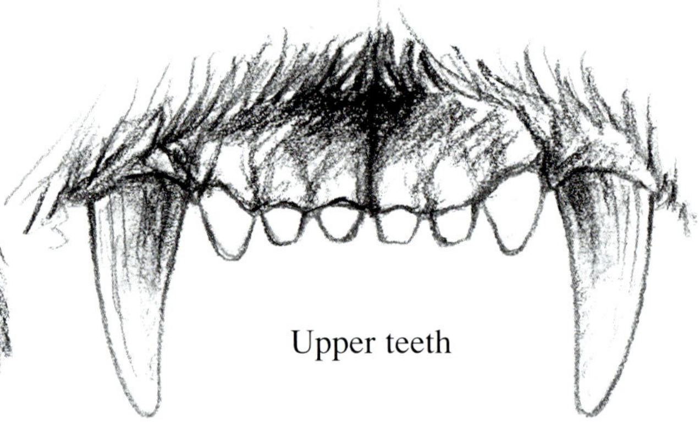

Upper teeth

ARTISTS: Drawing accurate animals means including the small (but *necessary*) details that often identify your animal. When possible (at zoos, in the wild, etc.) fill your sketchbooks with these *details* and then keep this reference material in your files for future use.

The diet of most Brown/Grizzly bears is about 90% vegetable (grasses, roots, berries, etc.) and therefore there is usually a lot of digging. Front claws are over 4" long and rear claws are about 2" long.

When I travel in the field, I often carry a field-pack of art materials, such as the items shown above. You may add or subtract things according to your needs and interests. However, always start with a bunch of *sharp* pencils!

Grizzly / Brown bears can be mellow and playful one second and aggressive and explosive the next. Bears need *their space* and anything intruding into this space is doing so at its own peril.

Grizzly / Brown bears have lost over 90% of their original range here in North America. In the 1800's, the bears roamed across the continent from Alaska to Mexico. Today, however, the great majority of the estimated 40,000 bears are confined to Alaska and Canada. Fewer than 1,000 still roam in the lower 48 states of America.

the BLACK BEAR in Alaska

Alaska Department of Fish and Game
Wildlife Notebook Series

BLACK BEARS (*Ursus americanus*) are the most abundant and widely distributed of the three species of North American bears. They have been recorded in all states except Hawaii. In Alaska, black bears occur over most of the forested areas of the state. They are not found on the Seward Peninsula, on the Yukon-Kuskokwim Delta, or north of the Brooks Range. They also are absent from some of the large islands of the Gulf of Alaska, notably Kodiak, Montague, Hinchinbrook and others, and from the Alaska Peninsula beyond the area of Lake Iliamna. In Southeast Alaska, black bears occupy most islands with the exceptions of Admiralty, Baranof, Chichagof, and Kruzof. These are inhabited by brown bears. Both species occur on the southeastern mainland. Black bears are most often associated with forests, but depending on the season of the year, they may be found from sea level to alpine areas.

GENERAL DESCRIPTION: Black bears are the smallest of the North American bears. Adult bears stand about 29 inches (.73 m) at the shoulders and measure about 60 inches (1.5 m) from nose to tail. The tail is about two inches long. Males are larger than females. An average adult male in spring weighs about 180-200 pounds (81.8 to 90.9 kg). They are considerably lighter when they emerge from winter dormancy and may be 20 percent heavier in the fall when they are fat.

The color of this bear over its entire range varies from jet black to white. A very rare white or creamy phase occurs on Kermode Island and vicinity in British Columbia. Three colors are common in Alaska. Black is the most often encountered color, but brown or cinnamon bears are often seen in southcentral Alaska and the southeastern mainland. The rare blue (glacier) phase may be seen in the Yakutat area and has been reported in other parts of Southeast Alaska. Only the black color phase is seen on the islands of Southeast. Black bears may have a patch of white hair on the fronts of their chests.

Black bears are most easily distinguished from brown bears by their straight facial profile and their claws which are sharply curved and seldom over 1 1/2 inches in length. Positive identification can be made by measuring the upper rear molar which is never more than 1 1/4 inches long in the black bear and is never less than that in a brown bear. Black bears have adequate senses of sight and hearing. They do have, however, an outstanding sense of smell.

LIFE HISTORY: Mating can take place anytime from June through July. Apart from that time, black bears are usually solitary, except for sows with cubs. The fertilized egg will not implant in the uterus until the fall. The cubs are born in their dens following a gestation period of about seven months. The cubs are born blind, nearly hairless, and weigh under a pound. Upon emerging from the den in May, they may weigh about 5 pounds (2.3 kg) and are covered with fine wooly hair. They are able to follow their mothers quite well. One to four cubs may be born, but two is most common. Cubs apparently remain with their mothers through the first winter following birth. Bears mature sexually at 3 to 6 years of age, depending upon their environment. In their more southern ranges they will breed every other year unless a litter is lost early during the first summer, then the sow will breed again that year. In more marginal environments such as northern Alaska, black bears keep their cubs with them an extra year and will breed every third year.

FOOD HABITS: Black bears are creatures of opportunity when it comes to food. There are, however, certain patterns of food-seeking which they follow. Upon emergence in the spring, freshly sprouted green vegetation is their main food item, but they will eat nearly anything they encounter. Winter-killed animals are readily eaten, and in some areas black bears have been found to be effective predators on newborn moose calves. As summer progresses, feeding shifts to salmon if they are available. In areas without salmon, bears rely primarily on vegetation throughout the year. Berries, especially blueberries, are an important late summer-fall food item. Ants, grubs, and other insects help to round out the black bear's diet. Male bears may occasionally prey on their own young.

WINTER DORMANCY: As with brown bears, black bears spend the winter months in a state of hibernation. Their body temperatures drops, their metabolic rate is reduced, and they sleep for long periods. Bears enter this dormancy period in the fall, after most food items become hard to find. They emerge in the spring when food is again available. Occasionally, in the more southern ranges, bears will emerge from their dens during winter. In the northern part of their range, bears may be dormant for as long as seven to eight months. Females with cubs usually emerge later than lone bears. Dens may be found from sea level to alpine areas. They may be located in rock cavities, hollow trees, self-made excavations, even on the ground.

HUMAN USE: At one time black bears were classified as furbearers and were heavily used as such. Now there is a growing appreciation for them as a meat and trophy animal. Black bears are so common and widely distributed that they often cause damage at homesteads, construction camps, or even in towns and are destroyed as nuisance animals. These depredation kills can be minimized or eliminated if garbage and other food items which attract bears to camps or residences are eliminated. In some areas of Alaska, black bears are a traditional subsistence food. In the community of Huslia, for instance, hibernating bears are killed, cooked, and eaten by the men and boys of the community in a traditional dinner.

The best bear hunting areas are probably from the tidal areas in Prince William Sound southward through the panhandle of Alaska. In these areas, bears are spotted from boats as they forage on the beach. Early May through early June is usually the best time for such hunting. The pelts of spring black bears make beautiful trophies if taken before they start to rub.

If bear flesh is used for human food, it must be well cooked as Alaska bears have been known to have trichinosis. This disease is transmitted by eating infected meat that is not cooked thoroughly.

DANGER TO HUMANS: Bears are extremely powerful animals and potentially dangerous to humans. They are usually highly cautious and secretive, but if they have a food supply, they may defend it against all intruders. Every year, bears are found in Alaska's biggest cities—in downtown Juneau, Anchorage, and Fairbanks. Encounters with humans frequently occur especially near garbage dumps and fish drying racks. Sows with cubs must always be respected. A rule of thumb is never to come between or near a mother bear and her young.

Normally, these bears snort in a characteristic way and move off. They have, however, attacked without apparent provocation. Several persons have been victims of these unprovoked attacks. In general, all bears should be considered potentially dangerous and should be treated with respect. Black bears that appear unafraid of humans and allow people to approach closely should be treated with utmost caution.

Text: Loyal Johnson
Revised and reprinted 1994

Editor's Note: In some parts of the world, particularly Asia, certain parts of bears are highly desired for medicinal and ceremonial purposes. This demand has led to illegal hunting and marketing of bear claws, gall bladders, and other items. The pressure is great enough to jeopardize some bear populations, especially those whose numbers are low and whose habitat is restricted, and it is a significant threat to the future of bears everywhere. **In Alaska it is illegal to purchase, sell, or barter any part of a bear.**

Adult Black bear

Range of the Black Bear in Alaska (shaded area)

Black Bear Study

Black bear

A Black bear cub plays on a log.

135

Black bears have short, curved, retractable claws which allows them to be great tree climbers.

the POLAR BEAR in Alaska

Alaska Department of Fish and Game
Wildlife Notebook Series

POLAR BEARS (*Ursus maritimus*) are of special interest because of their large size, white color, and position as the top trophic level carnivore in the remote arctic environment. They occur only in the northern hemisphere, nearly always in association with sea ice.

GENERAL DESCRIPTION: Polar bears and brown bears evolved from a common ancestor and are still closely related, as demonstrated by matings and production of fertile offspring in zoos. Polar bears are similar in size to large brown bears. Adaptations by the polar bear to life on sea ice include a white coat with water repellent guard hairs and dense underfur, short furred snout, short ears, teeth specialized for a carnivorous rather than an omnivorous diet, and hair nearly completely covering the bottom of the feet. Cubs weigh between 1 and 2 pounds (0.5-0.9 kg) at birth. An extremely large adult male may weigh 1,500 pounds (680 kg). Most mature males weigh between 600 and 1,200 pounds (273-545 kg) and are between 8 and 10 feet (2.4-3.0 m) in length. Mature females weigh 400 to 700 pounds (182-318 kg).

LIFE HISTORY: Polar bears, other than family groups of females and young, are solitary most of the year. During the breeding season in late March, April, and May, males actively seek out females by following their tracks on the sea ice. Bears are polygamous, and the male remains with a receptive female a relatively short time and then seeks another female. Pregnant females seek out denning areas in late October and November. Denning occurs on land and on sea ice. A denning female excavates a depression in the snow under a bank, on a slope, or near rough ice. She enlarges the denning chamber as drifting snow accumulates in depth. Young are born in the den in December. A litter of two is the most common. The female and cubs emerge from the den in late March or early April when cubs weigh about 15 pounds (6 . 8 kg). They make short trips to and from the open den for several days as the cubs become acclimated to outside temperatures. They then start traveling on the drifting sea ice. Young most commonly remain with the mother until they are about 28 months old. Females can breed again at about the same time they separate from their young, so normally they can produce litters every third year. Bears in the wild have been recorded as old as 32 years, but most probably do not live beyond 25 years.

DISTRIBUTION AND MIGRATION: Polar bears are most abundant near coastlines and the southern edge of the ice, but they can occur throughout the polar basin. They make extensive movements related to the seasonal position of the ice edge. In winter, bears off Alaska commonly occur as far south as St. Lawrence Island and may even reach St. Matthew Island and the Kuskokwim Delta. During the summer, bears occur near the edge of the pack ice in the Chukchi Sea and Arctic Ocean, mostly between 70° and 72° north latitude. Pregnant females concentrate for winter denning on Wrangel Island and other Russian islands, islands in the Canadian arctic, Greenland, and Spitsbergen. Some denning occurs along the north Alaska coast, especially within the Arctic National Wildlife Refuge, and on the adjacent sea ice. Mark and recapture studies indicate that there are several populations of polar bears in the polar basin that have relatively little interchange with one another. Off Alaska there are two populations. The Beaufort Sea population occurs along the North Slope of Alaska and ranges into western Canada. The Chukchi population occurs off western Alaska, with its range extending to Wrangel Island and eastern Siberia.

FOODS: The main food of polar bears adjacent to Alaska is the ice-inhabiting ringed seal. Bears capture seals by waiting for them at breathing holes and at the edge of leads or cracks in the ice. They also stalk seals resting on top of the ice and catch young seals by breaking into pupping chambers in snow on top of the ice in the spring. Bears prey to a lesser extent on bearded seals, walruses, and beluga whales. They also feed on carrion, including whale, walrus, and seal carcasses they find along the coast. They occasionally eat small mammals, bird eggs, and vegetation when other food is not available. A keen sense of smell, extremely sharp claws, patience, strength, speed, and the camouflaging while coat aid in procuring food.

HUMAN USES: Polar bears occur in areas under the jurisdiction of five nations - Russia, Norway, Denmark, Canada, and the United States - and also on the high seas where jurisdiction is not clearly defined.

In Alaska prior to the late 1940s, nearly all polar bear hunting was by Eskimos with dog teams. Sport hunting, sometimes with the use of aircraft, started in the late 1940s and continued through 1972. In 1972 the state of Alaska prohibited the use of aircraft in polar bear hunting. With the passage of the Statehood Act, Alaska began a polar bear management program. State regulations required sealing of skins, provided a preference for subsistence hunters, and protected cubs and females with cubs.

The federal Marine Mammal Protection Act (MMPA) of 1972 transferred management authority from the state to the federal government and placed a moratorium on hunting of marine mammals by people other than Alaska Natives. This resulted in a reduced total harvest but an increase in the proportion of female bears and cubs. The MMPA includes provisions that allow for waiver of the moratorium or transfer of management authority back to states. At intervals since 1972, the State of Alaska has made efforts at regaining polar bear management. State management could allow a resumption of sport hunting and produce increased economic opportunities in coastal rural communities. For a variety of reasons, efforts to regain state management have been discontinued. Polar bear meat, other than that of males in the rut, is quite palatable when boiled. It is a favored subsistence food in some areas. Meat should be cooked thoroughly before eating as polar bears have a high incidence of trichinosis, the round worm which occurs in pork and in other bear species.

Representatives of the five polar bear nations prepared an international agreement on conservation of polar bears in November 1973. The pact was ratified in 1976. It allows bears to be taken only in areas where they have been taken by traditional means in the past and prohibits the use of aircraft and large motorized vessels as an aid to taking. The agreement has created a high seas polar bear sanctuary but does not prohibit recreational hunting from the ground using traditional methods. In Canada, recreational hunting of polar bears currently provides significant economic benefits to Native people.

The stocks of polar bears in Alaska are shared with other nations, and national management programs should be coordinated. In 1988, the North Slope Borough Department of Wildlife Management (representing Alaska Natives) and the Inuvialuit Game Council (representing Canadians) signed an agreement to provide for coordinated management of the Beaufort Sea polar bear stock. Negotiations are currently underway between the U.S. and Russia for an agreement on management for the Chukchi stock.

Degradation of polar bear habitat is currently of more concern than effects of hunting on populations. Human activities, especially those associated with oil and gas exploration and extraction, pose the greatest immediate threat. Oil exploration and drilling activities in denning areas could cause bears to den in less suitable areas. Oil spills from offshore drilling and transportation of oil through ice covered waters could contaminate bears and reduce the insulating value of their fur, or adversely affect animals in the food chain below them. Severe environmental conditions would hinder or prevent containment of a spill, and currents and ice movement could distribute oil over large areas.

Text: Jack Lentfer
Revised by Lloyd Lowry and reprinted 1994

Range of the Polar Bear in Alaska (shaded area)

Female Polar bears normally give birth in November to January in a snug winter's den. These cubs, from one to four, will stay with their mother for about two years before she abandons them to breed again.

"Mamma's Sleeping"

Sow

Polar Bear Study

"Peaceful Arctic"

140

Polar bears are classified as marine mammals and are often observed swimming miles from land or ice while moving to new hunting territories. Large, front, paddle-like paws propel the bear through the water.

the ROOSEVELT ELK in Alaska

Alaska Department of Fish and Game
Wildlife Notebook Series

ROOSEVELT ELK (*Cervus canadenis rooseveltii*) herds present in Alaska originated from a transplant of eight calves captured on the Olympic Peninsula of Washington State in 1928 and moved to Afognak Island in 1929. Fossil bones indicate that a subspecies of elk once existed in Interior Alaska during the Pleistocene period. In North America, elk are sometimes called wapiti to distinguish them from moose (*Alces alces*) which are called elk in Europe. Roosevelt elk are larger, slightly darker in color, and have shorter, less symmetrical yet more massive antlers than the Rocky Mountain elk found east of the Cascade mountains in Canada and the United States.

Elk are found on Afognak and Raspberry islands near Kodiak. Elk were transplanted to Etolin Island near Petersburg in 1986. Previous transplants to Southeast Alaska were unsuccessful.

GENERAL DESCRIPTION: Elk are members of the deer family and share many physical traits with deer, moose, and caribou. They are much larger than deer, but not as large as the moose which occur in Alaska. Distinguishing features include a large yellowish rump patch, a grayish to brownish body, and dark brown legs and neck. Unlike some members of the deer family, both sexes have upper canine teeth. The males have antlers which in prime bulls are very large, sweeping gracefully back over the shoulders with spikes pointing forward. Alaska elk antlers have a tendency toward crowning, the formation of the three points at the end of each antler. Elk shed their antlers during the winter each year and grow new ones the following summer. The soft growing antler is covered with "velvet" which is scraped off by rubbing and jousting after the antlers harden in the fall.

Bull elk on Afognak Island are estimated to weigh up to 1,300 pounds (590.9 kg). Cow elk are similar in appearance to the bulls, but are smaller and have no antlers.

LIFE HISTORY: Elk calves are born in late May or early June when abundant food is available for the mother and the mild weather increases the calves' chances for survival. Birth usually occurs under the cover of dense spruce forests, hidden from predators and protected from the elements. Calves are born with protective coloration (light spotted areas on the back which act as camouflage). A few days after giving birth, the mother joins other cow elk with calves. A single cow will often "babysit" with the calves while the remaining cows seek food. As summer progresses, elk bands move above timberline and feed on the alpine slopes where breezes keep biting insects at bay and young plants are highly nutritious. By July, the calves, although still nursing, begin feeding on succulent forbs.

Beginning in August, bands of elk congregate and form herds consisting of cows, calves, yearlings and an occasional mature bull. Nearby, but separate from the herd, can be found small bands of mature bulls. During September, the bulls join the main herds and mating activities (the rut) begin. Large herds are scenes of vigorous activity as mature bulls challenge each other vocally, emitting a high pitched whistle or "bugle," an eerie but thrilling sound. Occasionally, pushing and shoving matches are initiated as the mature bulls attempt to take advantage of the larger bulls' preoccupation and run past them to win the favors of a female. By mid-October most breeding activities have ceased. The herds may begin to disperse into smaller bands as they move into wintering areas. The winter months are spent in lower valleys and in the dense spruce forests and small openings near the coastline searching for food.

FOOD: Elk are hardy animals whose large body size and herding tendencies require tremendous amounts of food. From late spring to early fall with a wide variety of food available, elk are mainly grazers, using grasses, forbs, and other leafy vegetation. By late fall they become browsers, feeding on sprouts and branches of shrubs and trees. The elk can become its own worst enemy as large herds often damage their food supply by excessive stripping, trampling, and overcropping staple food plants, including willow and elderberry. For this reason, it is important to keep elk herds from becoming too large in relation to the available food supply.

POPULATION: From the original eight transplanted animals, Afognak elk had expanded to approximately 1,200 to 1,500 animals by 1965. A series of hard winters with heavy snow accumulation during the late 1960s and early 1970s resulted in extensive natural mortality and reduced calf production and survival. By the mid-1980s the population had recovered to number about 1,200 animals. Factors which may limit the growth of elk populations include hunting, starvation, disease, predation by brown bears, and a lowered birth rate when the animals become too numerous to be supported by the available food supply. Timber cutting and the development of logging roads may result in further decreases in the area's "carrying capacity" for elk.

HUNTING SEASONS: Hunting seasons on Afognak and Raspberry islands were quite liberal during years of peak elk abundance in the 1960s, but even with a bag limit of two elk, the kill never exceeded 150 animals. After the extensive die-off in the late 1960s and early 1970s, some areas were closed to hunting and a more restrictive permit hunting system was imposed. These protective measures contributed to the recovery of the elk herds, and by the late 1970s all of Afognak and Raspberry islands were again open to hunting by permit. Hunters took a record of 271 elk in 1984. Steep terrain, heavy timber and predominantly bad weather make Alaska elk hunting a difficult and challenging pursuit.

Text: Sterling Eide
Revised and reprinted 1994

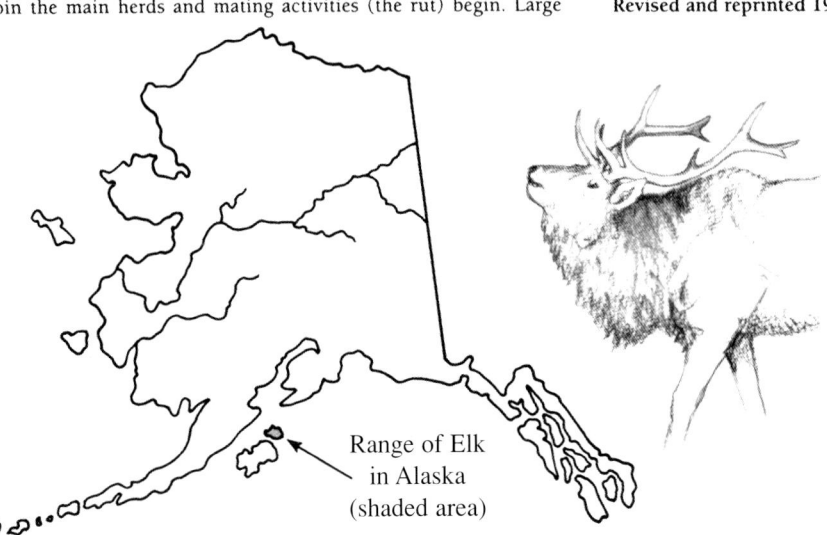

Range of Elk in Alaska (shaded area)

Roosevelt elk bull

Elk study

Elk Study

the SITKA BLACK-TAILED DEER in Alaska

Alaska Department of Fish and Game
Wildlife Notebook Series

The **SITKA BLACK-TAILED DEER** (*Odocoileus hemionus sitkensis*) is native to the wet coastal rain forests of Southeast Alaska and north-coastal British Columbia. Its range has been expanded by transplants, and established populations now also exist near Yakutat, in Prince William Sound, and on Kodiak and Afognak islands.

GENERAL DESCRIPTION: The Sitka black-tailed deer is smaller, stockier, and has a shorter face than other members of the black-tailed group. Fawns are born in early June and weigh 6 to 8 pounds (2.7-3.6 kg) at birth. The average October live weight of adults is about 80 pounds (36 kg) for does and 120 pounds (54.5 kg) for bucks, although dressed-weight bucks of over 200 pounds (90.1 kg) have been reported. The summer coat of reddish-brown is replaced by dark brownish gray in winter. Antlers are dark brown with typical black-tailed branching. Normal adult antler development is three points (including the eyeguard) on each side. They are relatively small, with very few scoring more than 110 points by the Boone and Crockett system.

Their average life span is about 10 years, but a few are known to have attained an age of at least 15.

LIFE HISTORY: Fawns are born in late spring. After the winter snow pack recedes, deer disperse; migratory deer move to high elevation alpine / subalpine habitats while resident deer remain at lower elevations throughout the forest. Summer and early fall are periods of active foraging as deer accumulate fat reserves which will help them through the winter and early spring. With the first heavy frost, deer in the higher alpine and subalpine areas descend to the upper forest.

The breeding season (or rut) peaks during late November. Breeding bucks spend little time foraging and by late November have used up much of their fat reserve. Does, however, generally enter December in prime condition. Does breed during their second year of life and continue producing fawns annually until they are 10 or 12 years of age. Reproductive success decreases rapidly beyond 10 to 12 years and by age 15, which is probably the maximum life expectancy, reproduction has essentially ceased. Prime age does (5 to 10 years) typically produce two fawns annually.

Throughout the rest of the winter and early spring, deer are generally restricted to uneven-aged oldgrowth forest below 1,500 feet in elevation. The oldgrowth forest provides optimal winter habitat because the high broken canopy intercepts much snow but still provides enough light for the growth of forage plants used by deer. During winter, the distribution of deer at various elevations is influenced by changing snow depth. During extreme snow accumulation, many deer congregate in heavily timbered stands at lower elevations, and some may even move onto the beach. Spring is critical period for deer, and if winter snows are deep and persistent, many deer die of starvation. As snow melts in mid- to late spring deer begin to disperse, and by late spring and early summer they start rebuilding some of the fat reserves lost during winter.

HOME RANGE: Summer and winter home range areas vary from 30 to 1,200 acres and average about 200 acres for radio-collared deer on Admiralty Island. Migratory deer have larger annual home ranges than resident deer. The average distance between summer and winter home ranges is five miles for migratory deer and half a mile for resident deer. Movement of deer between watersheds appears to be minimal during winter.

FOOD HABITS: During summer, deer generally feed on herbaceous vegetation and the green leaves of shrubs. During winter, they are restricted to evergreen forbs and woody browse. When snow is not a problem, evergreen forbs such as bunchberry and trailing bramble are preferred. During periods of deep snow, woody browse such as blueberry, yellow cedar and hemlock, and arboreal lichens are used. Woody browse alone, however, is not an adequate diet and deer rapidly deplete their energy reserves when restricted to such forage.

POPULATIONS: Deer populations in Alaska are dynamic and fluctuate considerably with the severity of the winters. When winters are mild, deer numbers generally increase. Periodically, however, a severe winter will cause a major decline in the population. Deer have a high reproductive potential, and depressed populations normally recover rapidly. In some cases, however, predation may speed deer decline, as well as slow recovery to higher levels. The wolf, which occurs on the mainland and islands south of Frederick Sound, is considered the major predator of deer in Southeast Alaska. Both black and brown bears also prey on deer to some degree.

The most serious problem for deer management, however, is the permanent loss of quality winter range due to clearcut logging. Deer are highly dependent on uneven-aged old-growth spruce/hemlock forests. Current forest management practices allow clearcut logging in many areas throughout Southeast Alaska every 90-125 years . Although young clearcuts provide forage during snow free periods, forage is often unavailable in clearcuts during the winter months. More importantly, dense conifer growth in clearcuts will, in time, shade out all understory production, leaving very poor habitat for deer—a condition that persists 100 years or longer. In the long term, clearcut areas will experience a significant decline in deer numbers.

The presence of a number of parasites and disease has been noted in Alaska deer, with the lungworm being the most significant. Winter-killed deer often show signs of this parasite, particularly in northern Southeast Alaska. A high incidence of lungworm is frequently an indicator of high deer density, and lungworm infections probably contribute to deer mortality during hard winters. Lungworm is primarily a disease of animals of less than 2 years of age.

HUNTING: Throughout much of the range of Sitka black-tailed deer, normal, dispersed hunting pressure has little influence on deer numbers. Bag limits vary from complete closures to six deer of either sex, depending on populations. Early season hunting is concentrated in the alpine and subalpine areas. The largest portion of the harvest is taken in November during the rut when both sexes respond to a call resembling the bleat of a fawn. During late November and December, heavy snow sometimes concentrates deer at low elevations allowing high harvest levels when local weather conditions are favorable.

Text: Harry Merriam, John Schoen, and Dave Hardy
Revised and reprinted 1994

Fawn

A Sitka Black-tailed deer fawn plays in the fog.

Range of Sitka Black-tailed Deer in Alaska (shaded area)

Fawn

Buck / winter

Buck / late summer

Plains Bison bull

Wood Bison bull

the BISON in Alaska

Alaska Department of Fish and Game
Wildlife Notebook Series

AMERICAN BISON (*Bison bison*), which shaped the lifestyle of the Plains Indians and figured prominently in American history before they were brought to near extinction, were transplanted to Alaska from Montana in 1928. While bison were the most common large land mammal in Alaska thousands of years ago, all of Alaska's existing wild bison came from 20 animals released near Delta Junction. Natural emigration and transplants have now created additional herds at Copper River Chitina River, and Farewell. Small domestic herds are located at Healy, near Kodiak, and on Popov Island. There were approximately 700 wild bison in the state in mid-1985.

GENERAL DESCRIPTION: The bison is the largest native land mammal in North America. A full grown bull stands 6 feet (1.8 m) at the shoulder, is up to 10 feet (3.3 m) long and can weigh more than a ton (907.18 kg). Full-grown cows are smaller, but have been known to weigh over 1,200 pounds (544.3 kg). A bison's head and forequarters are massive and seem out of proportion to the smaller hind parts. Bison have a vertebrae which begins just ahead of the hips and reaches its maximum height above the front shoulder. From above the shoulder, the hump drops almost straight down to the neck.

The bison's horns curve upward. The horns of the bull are larger and heavier than the horns of the cow. In late fall, the bison's coat is a rich, dark brown. As winter progresses, the coat changes color and is much paler by spring. When the weather warms, the hair loosens and hangs in patches until it is completely shed and replaced with new hair by late spring. Hair on the chin resembles a goatee. Older animals tend to have more hair on their heads.

LIFE HISTORY: Most bison young are born in May, but calves are born from April to August or even later. Newly born calves have a reddish coat. They are able to stand when only 30 minutes old; within three hours of birth, they can run and kick their hind legs in the air. At about 6 days of age, calves start grazing. Their reddish-orange coat begins to darken at about 10 weeks, with the molt to dark brown complete about five weeks later.

Cows are sexually mature at 2 years of age and give birth to single calves twice in three years. The gestation period is approximately 270 days. On rare occasions, a mostly white or even albino calf has been born in the Delta herd, but none has ever reached maturity.

Bison in Alaska have been known to live to a relatively great age compared to other hoofed animals (ungulates). One tagged bull killed in the Copper River area was over 20 years old.

Bison are migratory animals by nature. Alaska's wild bison do not remain in single herds, but scatter alone or in groups ranging up to 50 animals or more. In the Delta Junction area, they move far up the Delta River in early spring to secluded meadows where they calve. Around August they travel back downstream, eventually moving onto the Delta Junction Bison Range; and finally in late fall, onto farms where they remain throughout the winter. Here they sometimes cause damage to unharvested crops. Alaska's other wild bison herds also have seasonal movement patterns.

Bison move slowly while feeding and appear to be quite clumsy. This is pure deception, for when pursued, the bison is fleet of foot and has great endurance. A mature bull eventually captured at Delta Junction jumped a seven-foot log fence from a standing position.

FOOD HABITS: Bison are grazing animals and in Alaska find only limited amounts of food along rivers, in recent burns, and sedge potholes. Their diet is made up mainly of various grasses and forbs like vetch, a favored summer food found on gravel bars. Sedges, silverberry, willow, and ground birch are also eaten. Good bison range is limited in Alaska, and it is unlikely that large numbers of bison can sustain themselves here as they did millennia ago.

HUNTING: To keep bison populations from burdening the limited carrying capacity of the range, to limit agricultural depredations, and to provide recreation and meat for sportsmen, controlled hunts are conducted each year. Hunters pursuing bison at Delta Junction, Chitina River, Copper River, or Farewell are often surprised by how difficult it is to stalk them. They are among the most difficult of Alaska's big game to bring down. The rewards of a successful hunt are a magnificent trophy and delicious meat which is similar to beef. The fat is edible, but is yellow rather than white and does not "marble" throughout the meat.

VIEWING OPPORTUNITIES: Photography and wildlife viewing enthusiasts will find the bison on their winter range in the Delta Junction area are fairly accessible, although respect and caution are urged when approaching this large animal. Bison are frequently visible throughout the summer at an overlook near Mile 242 on the Richardson Highway. Binoculars or a spotting scope are essential.

**"This information was excerpted from the Alaska Department of Fish and Game's Wildlife Notebook Series. For a copy of the complete series, call 907-465-4190 or write ADF&G, Division of Wildlife, P.O. Box 25526, Juneau, Alaska 99811".

Text: Bill Griffin and David M. Johnson
Revised and reprinted 1994

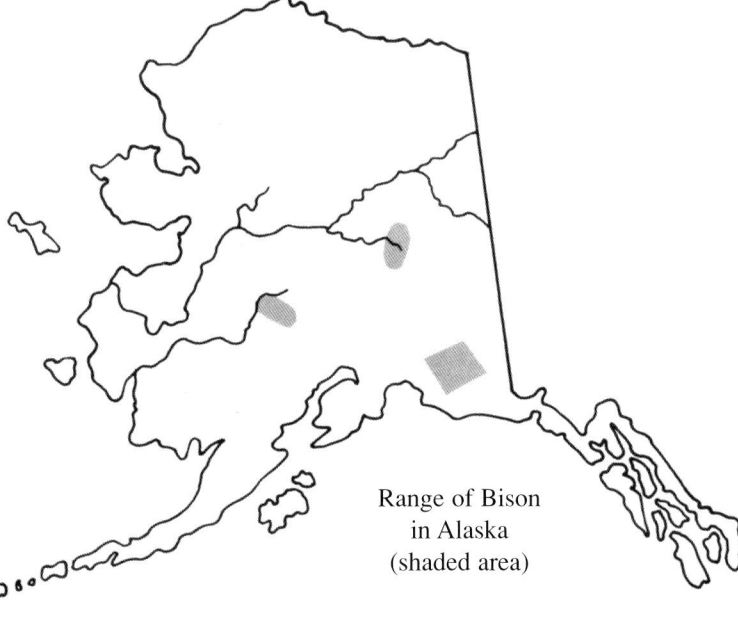
Range of Bison in Alaska (shaded area)

Plains cow and calf bison. A *rare* January birth. Calves are normally all born during the early spring in Alaska.

A Wood bison calf. Alaska is presently expanding a herd of imported Wood bison at the Alaska Wildlife Conservation Center near Portage, Alaska. Once this herd has reached a certain population, transplantations will be made into the wilds of Alaska; a place where they once roamed a hundred years ago.

the MOUNTAIN GOAT in Alaska

Alaska Department of Fish and Game
Wildlife Notebook Series

The MOUNTAIN GOAT (*Oreamnos americanus*) is the single North American representative of a widespread group of goat-like ungulates. All are characterized by relatively short horns and a fondness for living in rugged terrain. Because of its remote habitat. little was known about the mountain goat until almost 1900. Mountain goat hides had been obtained by Captain Cook as early as the late 1700s, but he had presumed that the specimens were of white bears, and the species was not described.

The mountain goat's range is restricted to the steep and broken mountain ranges of northwestern North America and extends naturally from Idaho and Washington to Southcentral Alaska. Mountain goat popopulations are scattered throughout this range and can be found from near sea level to over 10,000 feet, but some seemingly suitable areas are completely devoid of goats. In Alaska, mountain goats occur throughout the southeastern Panhandle and continue north and west along the coastal mountains to Cook Inlet. In Southcentral Alaska they are generally confined to the Chugach and Wrangell mountains, although their range extends into the Talkeetna Mountains nearly to Denali National Park. Mountain goats also have been transplanted to Kodiak and Baranof islands where they have established secure populations, to Chichagof Island where the transplant apparently failed, and most recently to Revillagigedo Island where they are doing well.

GENERAL DESCRIPTION: Mountain goats are one of the two species of all-white, hoofed, large mammals found in Alaska. They are often confused with young and female Dall sheep but are easily distinguished by their longer hair, deeper chest, and black horns. There is a crest of long, erect hair up to six or more inches in length along the spine, on the rump, and over the shoulders and neck. Long hairs on the legs give the animal the appearance of wearing pantaloons. A shaggy crop of hair hangs down from the chin and lower jaw. The pelage is much longer in winter than in summer. Both sexes have a crescent-shaped gland behind each horn that increases in size during the rutting season. The appearance of both sexes is much alike except that males are considerably larger than females. The horns of an average adult female are equal in length to those of an average adult male but are more slender. Sexes are extremely difficult to differentiate in the field unless the female is accompanied by a kid. Goats are usually quite docile, and their usual gait, even when alarmed, is a deliberate pace.

LIFE HISTORY: Throughout their lives mountain goats remain in or near steep, broken terrain, a behavior pattern which most likely evolved as a means of avoidance of predators such as wolves, bears, or cougars. Mountain goats mate in November and December. Billies (male goats) may wander considerable distances in search of receptive females (nannies). They do not collect harems, but some battling occurs as males often show puncture wounds, particularly on the rear quarters. Adult males are segregated from other age classes except during the rut. They may form small bachelor groups, especially in summer. Females with kids and immature animals are generally found in groups but may form larger nursery bands in early to mid-summer. Usually a single kid is born in late May or early June after a gestation period of approximately 180 days. Twinning occurs rarely but is more frequent following mild winters. Kids are precocious and can keep up with adults when only hours old and hardly larger than snowshoe hares. Nannies seek solitude prior to giving birth but soon join other nannies with newborn kids to form nursery flocks. Kids usually remain with their mothers until the next breeding season. Mountain goats may live 14 to 15 years, though most live less than 12. Many goats show healed wounds and missing teeth, indicating a high incidence of accidents, presumably from falls.

FOOD HABITS: Mountain goats are both grazing and browsing animals, depending on the particular habitat and season of the year. They normally summer in high alpine meadows where they graze on grasses, herbs, and low-growing shrubs. Most goats migrate from alpine summer ranges to winter at or below tree line, but some may remain on wind swept ridges. As winter advances and the more succulent species are frost-killed, the feeding habits shift to browsing. Hemlock is an important winter diet item, but feeding habits in winter are mainly a matter of availability.

HUNTING: Mountain goats are not particularly wary of hunters and rely on the security of the cliffy territory. Approaching within shooting range is not difficult if the hunter is able to negotiate the terrain. When possible, it is usually best to approach from above as goats are more alert to possible danger from below. Goat horns are not particularly impressive when compared to some of the other game species, but from the standpoint of physical hardship, spectacular setting, trophy judging, and difficulty of the terrain, the trophy billy goat presents a unique challenge. The pelt of a prime mountain goat killed in late fall or winter is a beautiful specimen.

Interest in goat hunting has increased in recent years. Goats are relatively abundant throughout their Alaska ranges, particularly in southeastern Alaska, but many goats live in areas that are beyond the reach of hunters. With increasing demand, hunting must be regulated by permit systems statewide to avoid localized overharvest in accessible areas.

Mountain goats can provide excellent meat for the table. As with other wild food animals, much depends on when and how the animal is killed. A nanny or billy of 3 years or less taken prior to the rigors of winter is outstanding meat. Adult billies, regardless of the season they are taken, are generally very tough, particularly so after the rut. An excellent way to use the meat of an adult goat is to grind it into hamburger or have it prepared as sausage or other similar meat products.

Text: Loyal J. Johnson
Revised and reprinted 1994

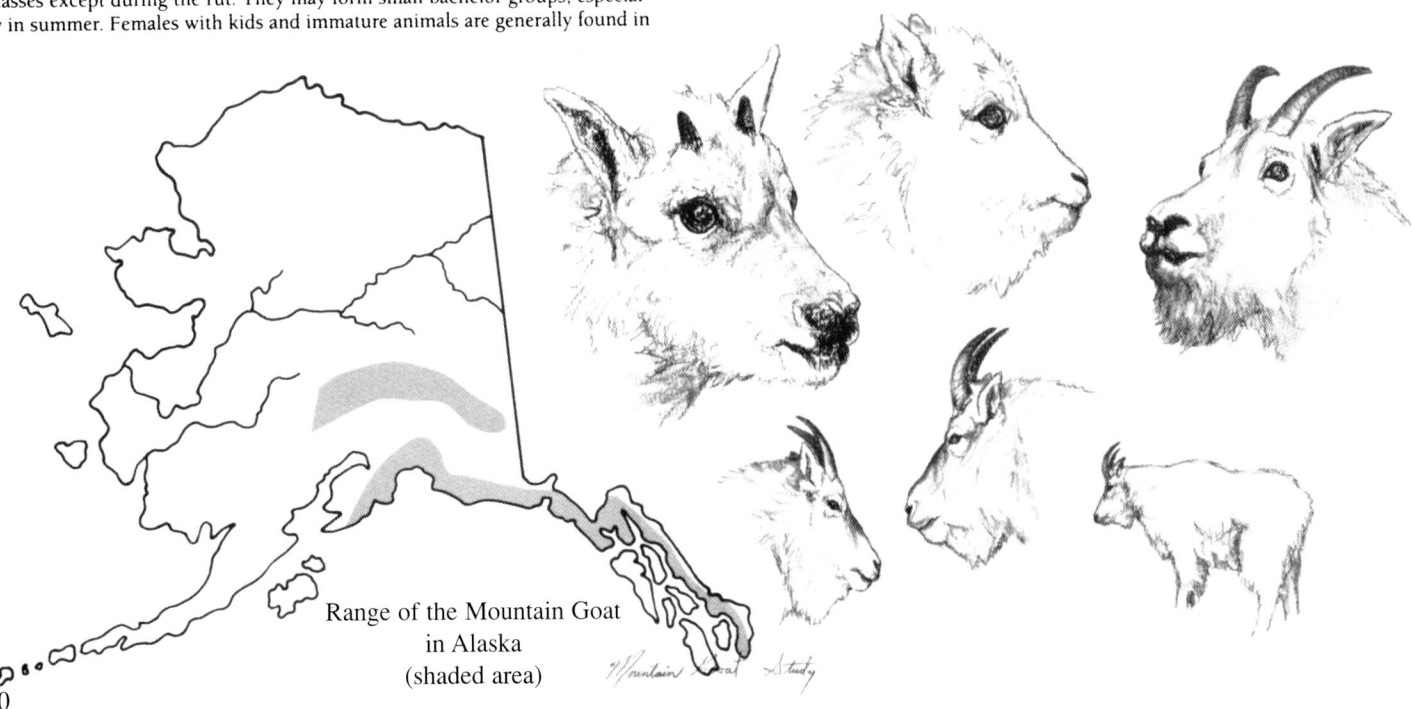

Range of the Mountain Goat in Alaska (shaded area)

Mountain Goats

Mountain Goat Study

Male Mountain Goats are called "billies".

Nanny & Kid (head)

Female Mountain Goats are called "nannies".

153

the MUSKOX in Alaska

Alaska Department of Fish and Game
Wildlife Notebook Series

The MUSKOX (*Ovibos moschatus*) is called *omingmak* meaning "the animal skin like a beard" by Inupiaq-speaking Eskimos, a reference to the long guard hair that hangs nearly to the ground. Taxonomists now classify muskoxen with the sheep and goats. The closest living relative of the muskox is the takin, a large goat-like animal which is found in the Himalayas. Muskoxen as a species have changed little since the ice age and are perfectly adapted to live in their harsh arctic environment.

GENERAL DESCRIPTION: The muskox is a stocky, long-haired animal with a slight shoulder hump and a very short tail. Both sexes have horns, but the horns of bulls are larger and heavier than those of cows. The horns of bulls develop large bases which nearly span the entire forehead. The pelage consists of a long, coarse, outer layer and a short, fine underhair. Coloration of the Greenland muskox, the race found in Alaska, is generally dark brown with creamy colored hair on the "saddle," forehead, and legs. Muskoxen have cloven hooves, all four of which are the same size.

Mature bulls are about 5 feet high (1.5 m) at the shoulder and weigh 600 to 800 pounds (273-364 kg). Cows are smaller, averaging approximately 4 feet (1.2 m) in height and weighing 400 to 500 pounds (182-227 kg). The name "muskox" is misleading because the animals have no musky odor.

LIFE HISTORY: The breeding season begins during late summer; mating takes place during the time from August to October. Single calves, weighing 22-31 pounds (10-14 kg), are born in the spring (April to June) to cows older than two years.

Growth is rapid and the animals weigh 150-235 pounds (68-107 kg) as yearlings. Muskoxen are gregarious animals. Winter herds may include up to 75 animals. Smaller harem groups, which form during the mating season, contain from 5 to 15 females and subadults, with one dominant bull who prevents other adult bulls from entering the group. Bulls excluded from these breeding herds wander widely in search of a harem but generally rejoin mixed-sex herds in winter. However, some non-breeding bulls may segregate into bull-only herds during spring.

Battles between bull muskoxen during the rut are spectacular and violent contests. After a period of aggressive display, the bulls charge at top speed from distances of 50 yards (46 m) or more and collide squarely on the horn bosses. The sound of the tremendous impact can be heard from a mile away on a calm day. After a clash, the bulls back away from each other swinging their heads from side to side and repeat the sequence until one bull turns and runs. A battle may include 20 clashes. Analysis of motion-picture footage has determined that the force generated in a clash between muskox bulls is equivalent to that of an automobile ramming a concrete wall at 17 mph (27 km/h). Bull muskoxen have heavily armored skulls to protect them from the shock of impact. Four inches of horn and three inches of bone lie directly over the brain in the area of contact.

The group defense formation adopted by muskoxen in response to predators is well known. When danger approaches, muskoxen run together. Every animal tries to face the source of the threat. If only one predator is nearby, the defense formation takes the form of a line. If several predators surround the group, as with a wolf pack, the formation becomes a compact circle with all muskoxen facing outward. Occasionally, one or more animals will charge the predator. The muskox's defense strategy is extremely effective against its principal enemy, the wolf. Unless the herd stampedes, it is nearly invulnerable to wolf attack. Early human hunters soon learned to exploit this defensive behavior and with the aid of dogs were easily able to wipe out whole herds of muskoxen. Whalers and arctic exploring parties, using the same techniques, took a heavy toll of muskoxen in some regions.

FOOD HABITS: Muskoxen eat a wide variety of plants, including grasses, sedges, forbs, and woody plants. Muskoxen are poorly adapted for digging through heavy snow for food, so winter habitat is generally restricted to areas with shallow snow accumulations or areas blown free of snow.

HISTORY IN ALASKA: The return of muskoxen to Alaska is an important success story in wildlife conservation. The original Alaska muskoxen disappeared in the mid- or late 1800s as they had much earlier in Europe and Asia. Overhunting likely contributed to their demise, at least in some areas. By the 1920s, muskox distribution was reduced to arctic Canada and East Greenland where a high take by whalers, hide hunters, and natives continued. Concern over the impending extinction of the species worldwide led to a move to restore a protected population to Alaska. In 1930, 34 muskoxen captured in East Greenland were brought to Fairbanks. In 1935 and 1936, all survivors and their calves were transported from Fairbanks to Nunivak Island and released. Muskoxen thrived on Nunivak Island and increased from 31 in 1936 to an estimated 750 by 1968.

Muskoxen from Nunivak Island were intended to provide stock for relocating animals to formerly occupied ranges. Nunivak Island muskoxen have been transplanted to the Arctic National Wildlife Refuge, Cape Thompson, the Seward Peninsula, Nelson Island, and to Wrangel Island and the Taimyr Peninsula in Russia. Additional animals have been donated to zoos and other institutions.

Most of the transplanted animals quickly adapted to their new surroundings and increased. Further transplants may be considered in the future. However, dispersal from previously translocated herds will be the primary method by which future range expansion occurs.

POPULATION: In 1990, approximately 2,220 free-ranging muskoxen resided in Alaska: 500 on Nunivak Island, 220 on Nelson Island, 500 in northern Alaska, 130 in northwestern Alaska, 700 on the Seward Peninsula, 150 on the Yukon-Kuskokwim Delta, with an additional 105 animals in captivity in domestic herds, research herds, and the Alaska Zoo in Anchorage. The Nunivak Island and Nelson Island populations have been stabilized by hunting; the other wild populations are expected to continue to increase and to expand their range.

POTENTIAL VALUE TO ALASKANS: Although the success achieved to date is impressive, the potential for future expansion is unparalleled. Although muskoxen were severely reduced in both numbers and distribution, their habitat has remained largely unchanged. It appears that habitat suitable for muskoxen is widespread, and given public support and proper management, muskoxen may eventually become a more visible and familiar wildlife species in Alaska.

Hunting of muskoxen under a limited permit system is conducted on Nunivak Island, Nelson Island, and in the Arctic National Wildlife Refuge. Muskoxen are considered a unique and valuable trophy. Muskox meat is highly valued among those who have tried it. This hardy survivor of the ice ages is an important attraction to tourists, photographers, researchers, and students of wildlife.

The soft brownish wool-like underhair, or qiviut, has been called the rarest fiber in the world. A domestic muskox herd at Palmer is farmed exclusively for the production of qiviut, but Eskimos on Nunivak Island collect the naturally shed wool clinging to bushes and tundra plants, and spin it by hand.

Text: Tim Smith
Revised by John Coady and Randy Kacyon, Reprinted 1994

Range of Muskoxen in Alaska (shaded area)

Bull muskox / winter storm

Three cow muskox / winter storm

Bull / summer

Muskoxen are truly hardy animals and are able to withstand the harshest weather that the arctic can dish out. Their warm underhair (or qiviut) is prized for its soft texture and is hand-spun to make scarves, hats and mittens that are sought after *Alaskan treasures*.

"Springtime in the Arctic"

155

the WOLF in Alaska

Alaska Department of Fish and Game
Wildlife Notebook Series

The WOLF (*Canis lupus*) occurs throughout mainland Alaska, on Unimak Island in the Aleutians, and on all of the major islands in Southeast except Admiralty, Baranof, and Chichagof. This range includes about 85 percent of Alaska's 586,000 square-mile area. Wolves are adaptable and exist in a wide variety of habitats extending from the rain forests of the Southeast Panhandle to the arctic tundra along the Beaufort Sea. Presently wolves are common over much of the state with densities as high as about one wolf per 25 square miles in favorable habitats. Densities are lower in the coastal portions of western and northern Alaska. Although the distribution of wolves has remained relatively constant in recent times, their abundance has varied considerably as prey availability, diseases, and harvests have influenced their numbers.

GENERAL DESCRIPTION: Wolves are members of the family Canidae. Early taxonomists recognized about 24 New World and eight Old World subspecies of *Canis lupus*, with four subspecies thought to occur in Alaska. Recent studies of skull characteristics, body size, and color suggest that differences are slight with considerable overlap in the characteristics of wolves from various areas. Only two Alaska subspecies are now recognized. Wolves in Southeast Alaska tend to be darker and somewhat smaller than those in northern parts of the state. The pelt color of wolves living in Alaska ranges from black to nearly white, with every shade of gray and tan between these extremes. Gray or black wolves are most common, and the relative abundance of each color phase varies over time and from place to place. Most adult male wolves in Alaska weigh from 85 to 115 pounds (38.6-52.3 kg), but they occasionally reach 145 pounds (65.3 kg). Females average 5 to 10 pounds (2-5 kg) lighter than males and rarely weigh more than 110 pounds (50 kg). Wolves reach adult size by about 1 year of age, and the largest wolves occur where prey is abundant year round.

SOCIAL HABITS: Wolves are highly social animals and usually live in packs that include parents and pups of the year. Larger packs may have two or three litters of pups from more than one female. Some yearlings may stay with the pack. The social order in the pack is characterized by a dominance hierarchy with a separate rank order among females and males. Fighting is uncommon within packs except during periods of stress, with the dominance order being maintained largely through ritualized behavior. Although pack size usually ranges from 2 to 12 animals, packs of as many as 20 to 30 wolves sometimes occur. The average size pack is 6 or 7 animals. In most areas wolf packs tend to remain within a territory used almost exclusively by pack members, with only occasional overlap in the ranges of neighboring packs. Wolves that are primarily dependent on migratory caribou may, however, temporarily abandon their territory and travel long distances if necessary. In Alaska the territory of a pack often includes from 300 to 1,000 square miles of habitat with the average being about 600 square miles.

LIFE HISTORY: Wolves normally breed in February and March, and litters averaging about five pups are born in May or early June. Litters may include from 2 to 10 pups, but most often 4 to 7 pups are born. Most female wolves first breed when 22 months old but usually have fewer pups than older females. Pups are usually born in a den excavated as much as 10 feet into well-drained soil, and most adult wolves center their activities around dens while traveling as far as 20 miles away in search of food, which is regularly brought back to the den. Wolf pups are weaned gradually during midsummer. In mid- or late summer, pups are usually moved some distance away from the den and by early winter are capable of traveling and hunting with adult pack members. Wolves are great travelers, and packs often travel 10 to 30 or more miles in a day during winter. Dispersing wolves have been known to move from 100 to 700 miles from their original range.

In spite of a generally high birth rate, wolves rarely become abundant because mortality is high. In much of Alaska, hunting and trapping are the major sources of mortality, although diseases, malnutrition, accidents, and particularly intraspecific strife act to regulate wolf numbers.

FOOD HABITS: Wolves are carnivores, and in most of mainland Alaska moose and/or caribou are their primary food, with Dall sheep being important in limited areas. In Southeast Alaska, Sitka black-tailed deer, mountain goats, and beaver are the most important sources of food. During summer, small mammals including voles, lemmings, ground squirrels, snowshoe hares, beaver, and occasionally birds and fish are supplements in the diet. The rate at which wolves kill large mammals varies with prey availability and environmental conditions. A pack may kill a deer or moose every few days during the winter. At other times, they may go for several days with almost no food. Since wolves are opportunistic, very young, old, or diseased animals are preyed upon more heavily than other age classes. Under some circumstances, however, such as when snow is unusually deep, even animals in their prime may be vulnerable to wolves.

MANAGEMENT: The food habits of the wolf often bring it into conflict with humans who in many parts of the world are also hunters of big game animals. Although the wolf has coexisted with big game animals for thousands of years, under some conditions the impact of predation contributes to local scarcities of game which, although temporary, arouse some people's concern. At other times, particularly in non coastal systems with moose and caribou, wolves serve an important role in maintaining game populations below levels at which their food supply would be damaged. As the myths that for so long dominated human thinking about the wolf have been dispelled, a remarkable change in attitude has occurred toward wolves in Alaska, and they are now considered a highly valued component of the state's fauna.

Various studies of wolf ecology have shown that the balance between wolf and prey populations is relatively fragile and can be easily disrupted. For example, severe winters may drastically reduce a big game population. Because many of Alaska's big game populations and their habitats are less productive than those in lower latitudes and because predators such as wolves and bears are still common here, human hunters will have to accept strict limitations on harvests from time to time. In some areas wolf numbers may need to be controlled in order to avoid relatively long periods of prey scarcity which could result in very low numbers of wolves and other furbearers.

Wolves can still be seen and heard in most parts of Alaska by those willing to spend time in remote areas. Although the future of the wolf in Alaska is reasonably secure, some challenges and problems remain. Will Alaska habitat remain available for large contiguous wolf populations as people expand their use of the land? The present attitudes of Alaskans and other Americans are cause for optimism, and wolves, humans, and big game animals should coexist indefinitely in Alaska despite some conflicts inherent in their relationships.

Text: Bob Stephenson
Revised by Rodney Boertje and reprinted 1994

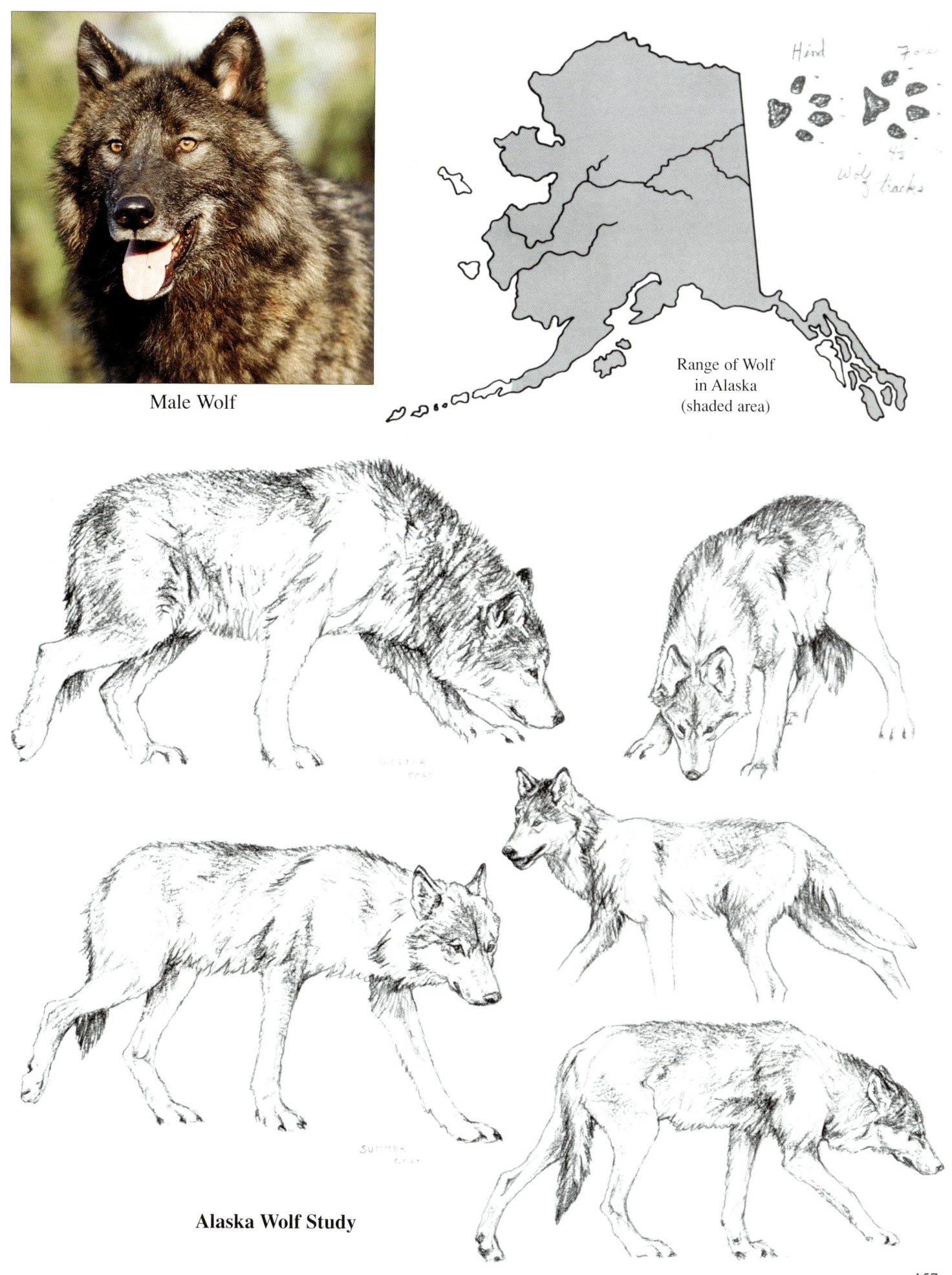

Male Wolf

Range of Wolf in Alaska (shaded area)

Hind Fore
Wolf tracks

Alaska Wolf Study

A male wolf runs down the gravel road in Denali National Park. This park is one of the best places to see wild wolves in Alaska because the road runs through vast areas of wilderness and because of the park's caribou herds. The park's wolves have been the subjects of various studies and numerous books.

"The Loner"

The wolf is surely one of the most *controversial* creatures in the world. Most people will either *praise* the wolf or spew out their *distain* for it. Few are undecided.

Alaska Wolf Study

Wolves normally mate for life and usually live in a social pack made up of parents and pups. Pack sizes vary, but 5-8 wolves is probably average. Pups are born in May/June in secluded den sites and by winter are able to travel and hunt with the adults.

Study

Pups

Wolf / Denali National Park

A dark-colored male wolf patrols the gravel road in Denali National Park. This curving road gives the wolves' easy access from one hunting or denning area to another. Also, road traffic (cars, trucks and tour-buses) often run over careless snowshoe hares and ground squirrels and the fox and wolves that travel the road will occasionally pick-up an easy meal.

Pups

Wolves are long-legged and seemingly tireless.

"On Golden Pond"

the COYOTE in Alaska

Alaska Department of Fish and Game
Wildlife Notebook Series

The wiley COYOTE (*Canis latrans incolatus*), so deeply rooted in the history and lore of the American West, is a newcomer to the Alaska scene. Coyotes were first noted in the state shortly after the turn of the 20th century. Populations were first reported on the mainland of Southeast Alaska, then slowly expanded northward into the upper Tanana Valley from which they radiated in all directions. A population peak occurred around 1940; since that time numbers have declined in many areas. There are few records of the coyote north of the Yukon River, although they do occur in that area. Portions of the state with the highest densities of coyotes are the Kenai Peninsula, the Matanuska-Susitna valleys and the Copper River Valley.

GENERAL DESCRIPTION: The coyote, like the wolf, is a member of the dog family and resembles a medium-sized shepherd-collie type dog. Distinctive features of the coyote are its sharp pointed ears that never droop, a sharp pointed nose, and long bushy tail. The legs of the coyote are generally slimmer and the feet smaller than those of a dog of comparable size. Coyotes average 22 to 33 pounds (10-15 kg) or about one-third the size of wolves. Males are slightly heavier than females. Coyotes average 2 feet high (.6 m) at the shoulder and, including tail, are approximately 4 feet (1.2 m) long. The summer coat is predominantly gray, washing into tan along the belly, lower legs, muzzle, and ears. Some guard hairs are tipped with black, as is the tail. The upper lip and underside are whitish. The intensity and amount of coloring varies, and individuals are usually lighter in winter.

FOOD HABITS: The coyote is best described as an opportunistic feeder. In Alaska, snowshoe hares, microtine rodents, and carrion comprise the bulk of the coyote's diet, while marmots, ground squirrels, muskrats, fish, insects, and even Dall sheep are taken in fewer numbers.

Coyotes hunt singly, in pairs, and occasionally in packs. They sometimes hunt cooperatively and have been observed using techniques such as chasing prey animals in relays, which allows them to capture animals that could outrun a single coyote. The coyote's method of capturing microtine rodents is similar to that of the fox. Upon locating its prey, the coyote makes a high, arching jump and pins the rodent to the ground with its forepaws. Often the prey is trapped under a mat of surrounding vegetation through which a more direct approach would be difficult.

Occasionally the coyote finds itself on the other end of the "dinner table." Great horned owls, bald and golden eagles, wolves, and bears all have been known to prey on coyotes . In some locations, free-ranging dogs will readily kill coyotes when the opportunity presents itself.

LIFE HISTORY: Coyotes breed in February and March. A mated pair may stay together through the spring and share parental duties after the pups are born. Other coyotes, especially young of the previous years, may also help care for the pups. Shortly before whelping, one or more dens are prepared for the litter. Coyotes give birth to an average of five to seven blind and helpless pups. The size of litters varies in response to the food supply. Litters born in times of plenty will, on the average, be larger than those born when food resources are scarce. For the first three weeks the young coyotes subsist entirely on milk. About this time some solid food regurgitated by the females is introduced into their diet, and the pups are weaned at 5-7 weeks. Once the pups establish a pattern of eating regurgitated food, they will induce the parents to regurgitate by biting and clawing at their lips. At the age of 3-3 1/2 months the pups are able to capture food for themselves.

Dens are used only for whelping the young and are abandoned during the remainder of the year. When a den is disturbed by humans, it is not unusual for coyotes to move the pups to another den. Family units may begin to break up as early as August, although it is not unusual for them to remain together into November or even later.

The coyote may be the most vocal of the canids and is sometimes referred to as the song dog. The most common call is a long, mournful, high-pitched howl which ends in a series of sharp yips and yaps. The howl of the coyote has a somewhat ventriloquistic effect, and it has often been reported that the howling of two or three coyotes sounds like a dozen or more animals are involved.

Like other canids, the coyote is susceptible to rabies, distemper, and other diseases which may cause periodic declines in coyote populations. Because of competition, coyotes are absent or scarce where wolves are abundant, and foxes are similarly less abundant where coyotes are numerous.

COYOTES AND HUMANS: In the wake of relentless expansion of humans into wildlife's domain, few species have been able to coexist and even expand their range as well as the coyote. The elimination or reduction of wolves from many areas of America, coupled with land and clearing activities, has contributed to this range extension.

The major source of the coyote's conflict with humans has been its fondness for sheep and poultry. Though only a few individuals are usually involved in such cases, massive predator control programs using poisons such as 1080 and strychnine, "coyote getters" loaded with cyanide, traps, aerial shooting, and bounties have been launched against the coyote. In many states these weapons were very effective, and numbers of coyotes were greatly reduced. Alaska was not left out of the program. The attitude toward coyotes was graphically demonstrated in a 1942-43 Annual Report of the Alaska Game Commission in which coyotes are referred to as "obnoxious animals." Today, attitudes about coyotes have changed radically. Bounties were removed in 1969, and the policy, as in other states, is one of control rather than extermination.

Today, a small number of coyotes are trapped each year, providing some income to Alaska trappers. In addition, a few are shot by hunters in pursuit of other species. A few individuals hunt coyotes by predator calling. The predator call simulates the cry of an injured rabbit and is probably the only effective way of hunting coyotes in Alaska.

The secretive nature of the coyote makes it an animal which is seldom seen by most Alaskans. It is for this reason that those rare sightings of a coyote take on a special significance. It appears that this newcomer to the Alaska scene, the "song dog of the West," has found a niche in our state.

Text: Donald A. Cornelius
Revised and reprinted 1994

Pup

Range of Coyote in Alaska (shaded area)

Winter coat / December

Adults (one yawning and stretching).

Pup

165

the RED FOX in Alaska

Alaska Department of Fish and Game
Wildlife Notebook Series

The **RED FOX** *(Vulpes vulpes),* is the subject of many stories, songs, fables, and parables. Its flashy good looks and its ability to live close to people and their varied activities have undoubtedly contributed to this notoriety. Probably a more important reason is the fox's reputation for cunning and intelligence. Several English similes testify to the fox's wily mind: "sly as a fox," "foxy," "outfoxed," and "crazy as a fox." Actually, the red fox has well developed senses of sight, smell, and hearing which are responsible for much of its reputation.

DISTRIBUTION: The red fox is common in most of northern North America. It is found throughout Alaska, except for some of the islands of Southeast Alaska, the western Aleutians, and Prince William Sound. It is native to Kodiak Island but is an introduced animal on many islands in the state as a result of fox farming operations in the early l900s. Red fox populations in Southeast Alaska are sparse, but the animal is found in the Taku and Stikine river valleys and the Mendenhall Flats. Red foxes have also been seen on Douglas Island near Juneau. The fox prefers broken country, extensive lowland marshes, and crisscrossed hills and draws. It is most abundant south of the arctic tundra. It is also present in tundra regions which it shares with the arctic fox. Where the ranges of the two species overlap, the red fox is dominant. In these areas, red foxes have been observed digging white (arctic) foxes from their dens and killing them.

GENERAL DESCRIPTION: Red foxes are members of the dog family Canidae, and their general appearance is similar to dogs, wolves, and coyotes. The European red fox is the same species as the American red fox. The red fox measures 22 to 32 inches (56-81.5 cm) head and body length, and the tail is 14 inches to 16 inches (35.5-42.5 cm). The adult fox weight is from 6 to 15 pounds (2.7-6.8 kg), but it appears heavier than it actually is. The males, or "dogs," are usually heavier than the females, or "vixens."

The red fox is usually recognized by its reddish coat, its white-tipped tail, and black "stockings," although the species does have many color variations. The outside of the ears may be black-tipped, while the inside is usually white. The white tip on the tail will distinguish this fox from other species, regardless of its color phase. Red is the most common color, but the hair may be from light yellowish to deep auburn red. Several color phases can occur in one litter. Red foxes displaying a distinct color pattern are referred by the name of that phase (i.e., red, cross, silver, black). The cross fox, for example, has a black/brown cross on the back and shoulders. The silver and black phases are similar. However, the black does not have the silvertipped guard hairs characteristic of the silver fox. The occurrence of black-silver phase appears to increase toward the north and the northwest of Alaska. However, even where most abundant, it comprises less than 2 percent of the population.

LIFE HISTORY: Red foxes breed during February and March. The den is a hole in the earth, 15 to 20 feet long, usually located on the side of a knoll. It may have several entrances. Sometimes foxes dig their own dens. More often, though, they appropriate and enlarge the homesites of small burrowing animals such as marmots. They also will use abandoned wolf dens. Conversely, wolves may enlarge and use a fox's den.

Within the den is a grass-lined nest where well-furred but blind babies, called kits, are born after a gestation of 53 days. A litter of four kits is common, though a litter of ten is not a rarity. At birth, kits weigh about 4 ounces. Normally only one litter is born each year. The kits' eyes open 8 to 10 days after birth. The young leave the den for the first time a month later. The mother gradually weans them, and by the time the kits are 3 months old, they are learning to hunt. Both parents care for the young. The family unit endures until autumn, when it breaks up and each animal is on its own.

FOOD: The red fox is omnivorous. Although it might eat muskrats, squirrels, hares, birds, eggs, insects, vegetation, and carrion, voles seem to be its preferred food. Foxes cache excess food when the hunting is good. They return to these storage sites and have been observed digging up a cache, inspecting it, and reburying it in the same spot. Apparently, they want to be sure that their food is still there.

IMPORTANCE: In areas where foxes have had little contact with humans, they display cautious curiosity. Even less fear is shown where contacts with humans are very common. Foxes are very adaptable to a wide range of habitat and can thrive close to humans, but they prefer wild settings. They require only a source of food and cover. Foxes are quite vocal, having a large repertoire of howls, barks, and whines. The red fox has several natural enemies: humans (principally as trappers), wolves, coyotes, lynx, wolverines, and perhaps bears. Eagles are the major predators of young foxes in some areas. In coastal areas from Dillingham to the North Slope, foxes are subject to periodic outbreaks of rabies which can kill all foxes in a wide area.

TRAPPING: Fox trappers have always respected the cunning displayed by this intelligent animal. Only the most carefully planned sets, free of human scent, will consistently catch foxes. Fox fur, like many other furs, fluctuates widely in popularity. When fox is out of style, the prices are correspondingly low. During the 1920s, when fox fur was fashionable, silver fox pelts sold for up to $500 each.

Text: Larry Jennings
Revised and reprinted in 1994

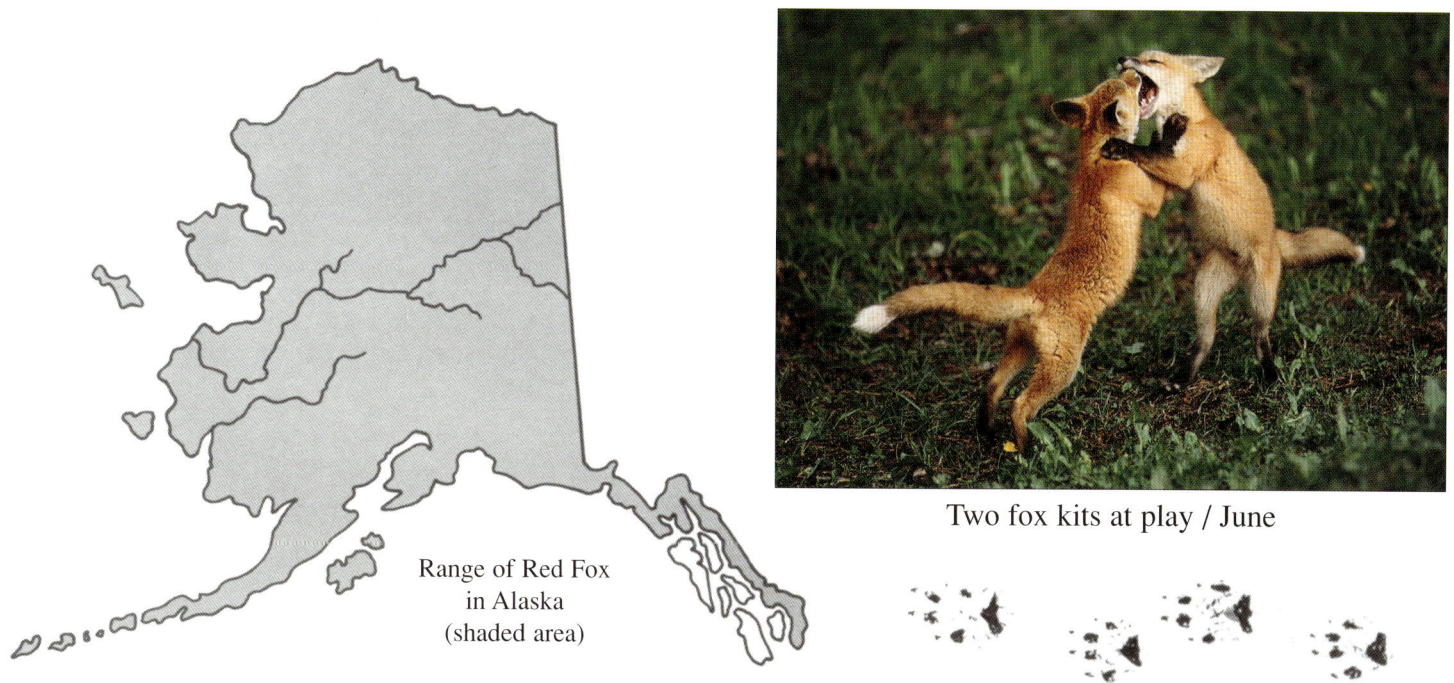

Range of Red Fox in Alaska (shaded area)

Two fox kits at play / June

Adult

A Red fox curls up in the snow. When dozing, the fox will usually bury his nose in his warm, fluffy tail.

A mother (vixen) Red fox greets one of her litter of five kits after returning to their den site.

"Red Fox Kits / Denali National Park"

A dark-colored Red fox carries an Arctic ground squirrel back to its den.

Red fox Study

A very young fox kit stands outside its den near McNeil Falls, an hour's flight out of Homer, Alaska.

A Red fox kit steals a golf ball off the 17th green at Eagleglen Golf Course in Anchorage, Alaska. This fox's family was denned beneath the boardwalk that spans a marshy area in front of the par-3 hole. Fox, eagles, moose and bears are routinely seen by golfers during their round of golf here on Elmendorf Air Force Base.

the ARCTIC FOX in Alaska

Alaska Department of Fish and Game
Wildlife Notebook Series

The **ARCTIC FOX** (*Alopex lagopus*) is found in treeless coastal areas of Alaska from the Aleutian Islands north to Point Barrow and east of the Canada border. Both blue and white color phases occur, with the blue phase more common on the Aleutian and Pribilof Islands. The white color phase is more common in northern litters. Young of each color phase may occur in the same litter.

GENERAL DESCRIPTION: Fully grown arctic foxes weigh from 6 to 10 pounds. They average 43 inches (1.09 m) in length including the tail. Their tails average 15 inches (38.1 cm) in length. Their short legs and body, short ears, and dense winter fur give them a stocky appearance compared to their relative, the red fox (*Vulpes vulpes*). Arctic foxes molt twice each year. The white foxes begin to shed their long winter fur in early April. By late June the face, legs, and upper parts of the body are covered with short, brown summer fur. The fur of the lower sides and abdomen is yellowish-white. The change to winter pelage occurs in September and October. By November the luxurious white winter coat is complete. Foxes of the blue phase remain dark or charcoal colored year round but become somewhat lighter in winter.

Newborn arctic fox pups of both color phases are covered with short velvety dark brown fur. This fur lengthens and becomes lighter, especially on the flanks, after the pups reach 2 weeks of age. The contrast between the back and belly increases as the back darkens during their first three months. Blue phase pups acquire their characteristic dark color by the time they are 2 months old.

LIFE HISTORY: Arctic fox pups are born in dens excavated by the adults in sandy, well-drained soils of low mounds and river cutbanks. Most dens have southerly exposure. They extend from 6 to 12 feet underground. Enlarged ground squirrel burrows with several entrances are often used as dens. Mating occurs in early March and early April. Gestation lasts 52 days. Litters average seven pups but may contain as many as 15 pups. Arctic foxes are monogamous in the wild. Both parents aid in bringing food to the den and in rearing the pups. Pups begin eating meat when about 1 month old and are fully weaned by 1 1/2 months. Pups begin to emerge from the den when about 3 weeks old and begin to hunt and range away from the den at about 3 months.

Family units gradually break up during September and October. During mid-winter, foxes lead a mostly solitary existence except when congregating at the carcasses of marine mammals, caribou, or reindeer. Arctic foxes attain sexual maturity at 9 to 10 months, but many die in their first year.

In summer, arctic foxes feed primarily on small mammals, including lemmings and tundra voles. Foxes denning near rocky cliffs along the seacoast often depend heavily on nesting seabirds such as auklets, puffins, and murres. When food is plentiful, it is sometimes cached among boulders and in dens for later use. Arctic foxes are omnivorous. They sometimes eat berries, eggs, and scavenged remains of other animals.

Many foxes venture out onto the sea ice during winter to eat the remains of seals killed by polar bears. Arctic foxes may move long distances over sea ice. A fox tagged along the coast of Russia was captured near Wainwright, Alaska, a year later.

In areas where lemmings and voles are the most important summer prey, numbers of foxes often rise and fall with cyclic changes of their prey. Fewer pups are successfully reared to maturity when food is scarce. There is evidence indicating that competition for food among young pups accounts for some of the heavy mortality in this age group.

HUMAN USE: Arctic foxes are abundant in many areas. Their numbers do not seem to be greatly affected by trapping. In the past 50 years, the annual harvest of white foxes in Alaska has ranged from a high of nearly 17,000 in 1925 to a low of 500 in 1956. The average is about 4,000 pelts per year. The demand for arctic fox fur has diminished in recent years, but the sale of their pelts is important to the economy of many coastal Native villages.

Arctic foxes are generally less wary of humans than their near relative, the red fox. They sometimes become nuisances around settlements. They are susceptible to rabies and can transmit this disease to humans. Foxes that approach humans without hesitation may have rabies and should be killed and submitted to health authorities.

**"This information was excerpted from the Alaska Department of Fish and Game's Wildlife Notebook Series. For a copy of the complete series, call 907-465-4190 or write ADF&G, Division of Wildlife, P.O. Box 25526, Juneau, Alaska 99811".

Text: Bob Stephenson
Revised and reprinted 1994

Tracks in snow

Study

Range of Arctic Fox in Alaska (shaded area)

Arctic Fox Study

Arctic fox / winter's coat

Arctic fox / summer's coat

the LYNX in Alaska

Alaska Department of Fish and Game
Wildlife Notebook Series

The **LYNX** (*Lynx canadensis*) is the only cat native to Alaska. Lynx occur over most of northern North America (though their numbers in the northern continental United States have been greatly reduced) and throughout Alaska except the Aleutian islands, Kodiak archipelago, the islands of the Bering Sea and some islands of Prince William Sound and Southeast Alaska. Because they are shy and unobtrusive animals, people think that lynx are scarce. In Alaska, however, they are commonly seen during long periods of summer daylight, especially during years that they are abundant. "Link" is a common local name for lynx in Alaska and the Yukon.

GENERAL DESCRIPTION: The lynx is a large, short-tailed cat, similar to the bobcat but distinguished by its long legs, furry feet, long tufts on the tip of each ear, and a completely black-tipped tail. The large, broad feet function as snowshoes to aid the lynx in winter hunting and traveling. The dense soft fur is buffy gray with indistinct spotting. Most adults weigh from 18 to 30 pounds (8.2-13.6 kg). Male lynx are generally larger than females and occasionally weigh 40 pounds (18.2 kg) or more.

LIFE HISTORY: Mating occurs in March and early April, and kittens are born about 63 days later under a natural shelter such as a windfallen spruce, a rock ledge, or a log jam. Lynx kittens resemble domestic cats at birth and are buff colored with longitudinal streaking on their backs. Their eyes open at about 1 month of age, and they are weaned when 2-3 months old. Most litters include two to four kittens, but sometimes as many as six are born and survive.

The production and survival of lynx kittens is influenced dramatically by cyclic changes in snowshoe hare and other small game populations. When prey are abundant, a high percentage of 1 year old or older female lynx produce kittens, most of which survive. When prey are scarce, very few yearlings breed, the number of breeding adults declines, and very few kittens survive until winter.

Kittens remain with their mother until late winter and acquire the hunting skills and knowledge necessary for their survival. During the following breeding season, family units begin to break up.

FOOD HABITS AND BEHAVIORS: Lynx inhabit much of Alaska's forested terrain and use a variety of habitats, including spruce and hardwood forests, and both subalpine and successional communities.

The best lynx habitat in Alaska occurs where fires or other factors create and maintain a mixture of vegetation types with an abundance of early successional growth. This provides the best habitat for snowshoe hares and other small prey of lynx. The primary prey of lynx in most areas is the snowshoe hare, which undergoes an 8-11 year cycle of abundance. This cycle appears to be caused by the interaction of hares with their food and predators. Lynx numbers fluctuate with those of hares and other small game but lag one or two years behind. When a hare population crashes, lynx numbers soon decline because of the small number of kittens reaching adulthood and the movement of some lynx out of the area. In recent studies of radio-collared lynx in Canada, Minnesota, and Alaska, movements of from 100 to 400 miles or more have been documented as lynx left areas where hares had become scarce. For example, a radio-collared lynx from the southern Yukon traveled over 400 miles to Chalkyitsik, Alaska.

Although snowshoe hares are an important prey for lynx, when they are scarce lynx use other food sources more extensively. Other small prey such as grouse, ptarmigan, squirrels, and microtine rodents are regularly taken. Lynx are also known to prey on caribou, Dall sheep, and foxes, especially during periods of scarcity.

Lynx normally travel 1-5 miles per day within home ranges ranging from 5 to more than 100 square miles. The largest ranges occur when prey are scarce. Lynx travel and hunt at a walk most of the time and capture their prey with short bursts of speed. They often ambush hares and other small prey while bedded down near small game trails. Lynx are adept at climbing trees but hunt mainly on the ground, sometimes using trees as a refuge from larger predators such as wolves.

Lynx are curious animals and are not difficult to trap using lures made from beaver castor, catnip, or other scents. Visual attractors such as bird wings or aluminum foil are often used to take advantage of the lynx's visual acuity. Since the early 1970s, lynx pelts have increased in value and may bring from $200 to $500. Their high value has led to increased trapping pressure and concern among trappers that lynx harvest should be regulated more closely. As a result, more restrictive seasons have been established in some parts of the state, with the goal of limiting harvest when lynx productivity and survival are low, thereby maintaining breeding populations that can prosper when prey are again abundant.

Text: Peter Berrle, Jeannette Ernest and Bob Stephenson
Revised and reprinted 1994

Lynx / Interior Alaska

Range of Lynx in Alaska (shaded area)

the WOLVERINE *in Alaska*

Alaska Department of Fish and Game
Wildlife Notebook Series

The **WOLVERINE**, a relative of the mink and weasel, is the largest terrestrial member of the family Mustelidae. Also known as devil bear, carcajou, or woods devil, its scientific name is *Gulo gulo*, meaning glutton. Wolverines occur in small numbers throughout their range and require large expanses of wilderness. Formerly distributed across most arctic and subarctic regions in North America, the wolverine has disappeared from most of the eastern United States and Canada. In Alaska, there have always been significant wolverine populations throughout mainland Alaska and some of the islands of Southeast Alaska.

The wolverine is valued by Alaskans as a fur resource and as a symbol of wilderness. Its fur is commonly used for parka trim and hoods because of its beauty and durability and because the guard hairs of wolverine fur resist frost accumulation.

GENERAL DESCRIPTION: The long dense fur of the wolverine is generally dark brown to black with a creamy white to gold stripe running from each shoulder along the flanks to the base of the tail. It has a thick body, short legs, short ears, and a broad flat head. The wolverine is primarily a scavenger and has large teeth and powerful jaws to crush bones and eat frozen meat. Adult males generally weigh 20-45 pounds (9-20 kg), while adult females weigh 15-30 pounds (7-14 kg). The wolverine's non-retractile claws are long and curved.

Wolverines are primarily found in the wilder and more remote areas of Alaska. They are solitary creatures throughout most of the year. Wolverines are active at any time of day, year-round. They have tremendous physical endurance and can travel up to 40 miles a day in search of food. Because of their great endurance and strength, wolverines have become a center of folklore. However, their fierce reputation has often been exaggerated. They have been known to steal furbearers from traps and to damage cabins, but these tales can normally be traced to individuals in some situations and not to the species as a whole. Wolverines will rarely attack any predator larger than themselves, like a wolf or a bear. Instead, they will try to avoid these animals. Wolverines will fiercely defend a food source or territory against other wolverines or smaller predators.

LIFE HISTORY: Wolverines become sexually mature in their second year. The breeding season extends between May and August. After wolverines mate, the embryo floats in the uterus until late fall or early winter. This type of reproduction is known as delayed implantation, and it allows a female wolverine to become pregnant when food supplies are best and when she is in good physical condition. Adults may fail to produce young in some years even if they had successfully bred. The abundance of food determines whether a pregnancy will be maintained and the number of young that will be born.

Wolverine litters are born between January and April. In Interior and northern Alaska, most young are born in snow caves. These caves usually consist of one or two tunnels that can be up to 60 yards long. No litters larger than four have been reported in the wild, and most are in the range of one to three. Baby wolverines, called kits, are born blind and weigh less than 1 pound (O . 5 kg). They develop rapidly and are weaned at about 8 weeks of age. They leave their mothers at approximately 5 or 6 months to forage for themselves. Wolverines attain most of their adult size and weight within their first year.

Wolverines travel extensively in search of food. Home range sizes are vast, with adult males using areas of up to 240 square miles. Adult females use smaller home ranges encompassing between 50 to 100 square miles. Adults maintain their home ranges more or less separate from those belonging to adjacent wolverines of the same sex. The home range of the resident male may encompass the ranges of up to four to six females. The breeding season is the only time during the year that males and females interact.

It appears that few wolverines live longer than 5 to 7 years in the wild. Some, however, do survive to 12 or 13 years of age . The primary natural mortality factors are starvation and being killed by other predators, primarily wolves. However, most wolverine mortality is due to trapping by humans.

FOOD HABITS: Wolverines are opportunistic, eating about anything they can find or kill. They are poor hunters but are well adapted for scavenging. The wolverine has a powerful jaw and large neck muscles, allowing it to crush and utilize bones and frozen flesh. Also, wolverines can survive for long periods on little food. Their diet reflects annual and seasonal changes in food availability. In the winter, wolverines rely primarily on remains of moose and caribou killed by wolves and hunters or animals that have died of natural causes. Throughout the year, wolverines feed on small and medium-sized animals such as voles, squirrels, snowshoe hares, and birds. In the right situations, wolverines can kill moose or caribou, but these occurrences are rare.

POPULATION MANAGEMENT: The continued health of wolverine populations in Alaska is best assured by both protecting large expanses of wilderness and preventing overharvest. Wolverines prefer vast areas of wilderness, and preservation of their habitat is of key importance to their successful management. Much wolverine habitat is now protected in the state through various federal and state land dedication programs. Harvests are controlled by seasons and bag limits. Annual catches and the effects on the population are closely monitored by the Alaska Department of Fish and Game to ensure that harvest by humans will not be a negative factor on Alaska's wolverine populations.

Text: Ken Taylor
Revised by Craig Gordon and reprinted 1994

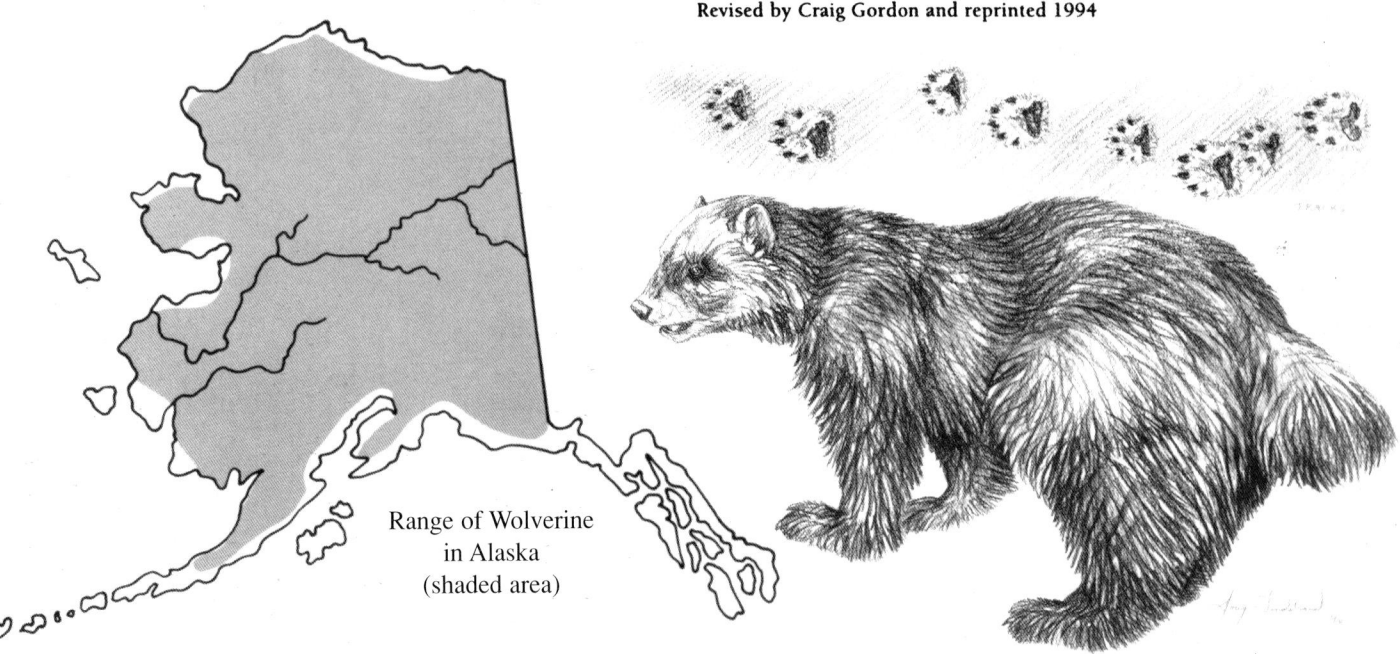

Range of Wolverine in Alaska (shaded area)

Wolverine Study

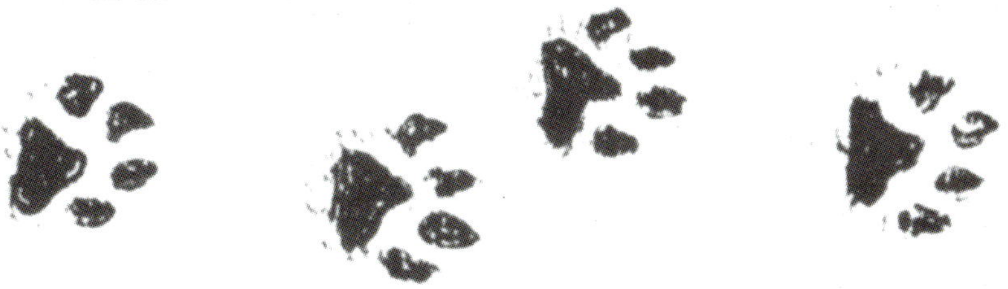

Adult

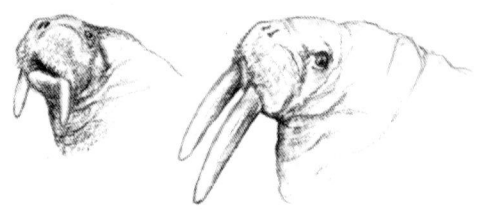
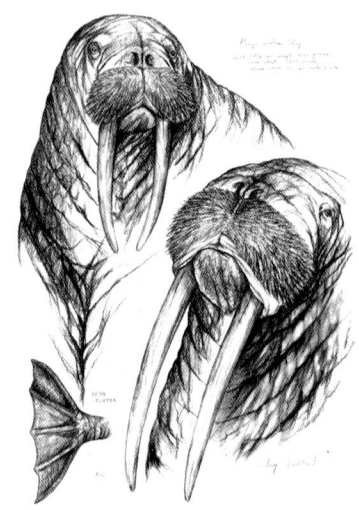

the WALRUS in Alaska

Alaska Department of Fish and Game
Wildlife Notebook Series

WALRUSES are members of a widely distributed group of marine animals known as pinnipeds (*pinna*, a wing or fin; and *pedis* a foot), a group which also includes the seals and sea lions. Walruses are the largest pinnipeds in arctic and subarctic seas. They are most commonly found in relatively shallow water areas, close to ice or land. Their geographic range completely encircles the Polar Basin. Two forms are presently recognized: the Pacific walrus (*Odobenus rosmarus divergens*) and the Atlantic walrus (*Odobenus rosmarus rosmarus*). The principal differences between the two are in the longer tusks and larger body size of the Pacific walrus. The groups may be regarded as closely related but geographically separated subspecies.

Today there are far more Pacific than Atlantic walruses. The 1990 population of the Pacific subspecies was estimated at about 201,000 animals. They are the mainstay of several Eskimo villages. Their flesh is used for food and the skins as boat coverings. The intestines were traditionally used to make rain gear. In the American sector of the Bering and Chukchi seas, walruses occur seasonally from Bristol Bay to Point Barrow. Most of the animals undertake a northward spring migration and return south during the fall. These movements are directly related to the seasonal advance and retreat of the sea ice. About 12,000 to 16,000 bulls remain in the Bristol Bay area from March through October. These males migrate northward in the fall to the St. Lawrence Island area, where they join the rest of the herd to spend the winter and spring in the ice pack.

GENERAL DESCRIPTION: The genus name for the walrus, *Odobenus* (meaning tooth-walker), refers to one of their most prominent characteristics, their tusks. These tusks, which are elongated upper canine teeth, are present in both males and females. The body form is basically like a sea lion, and they have flexible hind flippers that can be rotated forward, a thick, heavy neck, and a broad muzzle that bears a heavy, bristly moustache. They are huge animals. Adult bulls often approach 2 tons in weight, and the females may exceed 1 ton. Adult bulls can be recognized by their larger size, broad muzzle, heavy tusks, and the presence of numerous large bumps on the neck and shoulders.

LIFE HISTORY: Walrus calves are born mostly in late April or early May during the spring migration. They weigh 100 to 160 pounds (45-73 kg) at birth. Calves are dependent upon their mothers for at least 18 months and occasionally for as long as 2 1/2 years. Most females do not begin to breed until 6 or 7 years of age. Mating occurs during January and February, but growth of the fetus does not begin until about mid-June. This delay in fetal growth is thought to occur in all pinnipeds. The total gestation period, from conception to birth, is about 15 months. However, the actual period of fetal growth is about 11 months. Most cows do not breed again until the year following the birth of their last calf. Thus, calves are produced in alternate years by females in their prime. Calves are produced less frequently by the older females.

By 2 years of age, the young weigh about 750 pounds (341 kg). When the females are 11 or 12 years old, they weigh approximately 2,000 pounds (909 kg), their maximum weight. The males continue growing until at least 14 to 16 years of age.

The age of an individual walrus (except for very old animals) can be determined by the number of rings or "annual layers" observed in cross-sections of the teeth. In the older animals, some of the rings laid down during the first few years of life are worn away. However, examination of teeth has shown that walruses can reach the age of 40 years. Due to rather constant, significant, and selective hunting pressure, as well as other factors, it is doubtful that very many walruses die of old age.

FOOD HABITS: Walruses feed mainly on bottom dwelling invertebrates found on the relatively shallow and rich Bering-Chukchi Platform. Major food items include several different kinds of clams. Only the fleshy parts are eaten. It is believed that these parts are torn away from the rest of the clam by strong suction, a method of feeding for which the mouth of the walrus is ideally designed. The mouth of a walrus is narrow, with an unusually high roof, strong thick lips which are not deeply cleft along the side of the face (the gape is extremely limited), and a thick piston-like tongue. The tusks are probably not used to any great extent during feeding. The rejected shells can be found on the sea floor alongside the holes and furrows made by feeding animals. Other food items include snails, crabs, shrimps, worms, and occasionally seals. Walruses usually find food by brushing the sea-bottom with their broad, flat muzzles.

BEHAVIOR: The tusks are used for fighting, for climbing on both land and ice, and for emergencies of various kinds. A female walrus was observed literally demolishing a heavy piece of ice to free her calf, which had fallen into a crevasse. The tusks were as effective as a pick-axe. The presence of 12 men within 30 feet did not distract her from her task. Attempts to assist her in her efforts were met by furious charges and a threatening noise made by rapidly opening and closing her mouth. The noise sounded much like someone banging a pipe with a hammer. In due time she freed her calf and swam off, carrying it on her back.

Cows will not abandon their calves, and vice versa. The cows make every effort to rescue their offspring. They often carry their dead calves away from the hunters. Walruses, especially young males, will push dead and badly wounded animals (often larger than themselves) off an ice floe, out of the reach of the hunters. They will frequently return to an ice floe for as long as wounded animals continue to bellow. This sometimes places both people and boats in jeopardy. The return is not a reprisal attack but an attempt to lead the wounded animals to safety. A person imitating the sounds of a walrus can frequently get them to return.

Walruses (with the exception of some young bulls) are usually not malicious, but their inquisitiveness, size, and great strength demand caution of those who approach them.

Tusks are used a great deal in mutual display, with the strongest animals (usually with the largest tusks) being dominant over the others. When animals on an ice floe are disturbed, which happens frequently, they will raise their heads high, prominently showing their tusks. Animals with smaller tusks will usually move away or become respectfully quiet. The only serious battles (and these are quite brutal) are between animals of the same body and tusk size.

HUNTING: Walrus hunting is conducted from all of the Eskimo villages near which the animals occur. However, the bulk of the annual harvest is taken from the villages in and near Bering Strait, mainly Gambell, Savoonga, Nome/King Island, and Little Diomede Island. Hunting loss can be high. Several thousand animals are killed annually in Alaska. Some walruses are also taken by Siberian Eskimos and by Russian commercial hunting vessels.

The most favorable period for hunting walrus is during the spring and summer when the animals are passing the villages on their way north. Hunting is good on St. Lawrence Island during May, and progressively later at the most northerly locations. Walruses reach the vicinity of Wainwright and Barrow during late July or early August.

Text: John J. Burns
Revised and reprinted 1994

Pacific Walrus

Pacific Walrus

Pacific Walrus

Harbor Seal

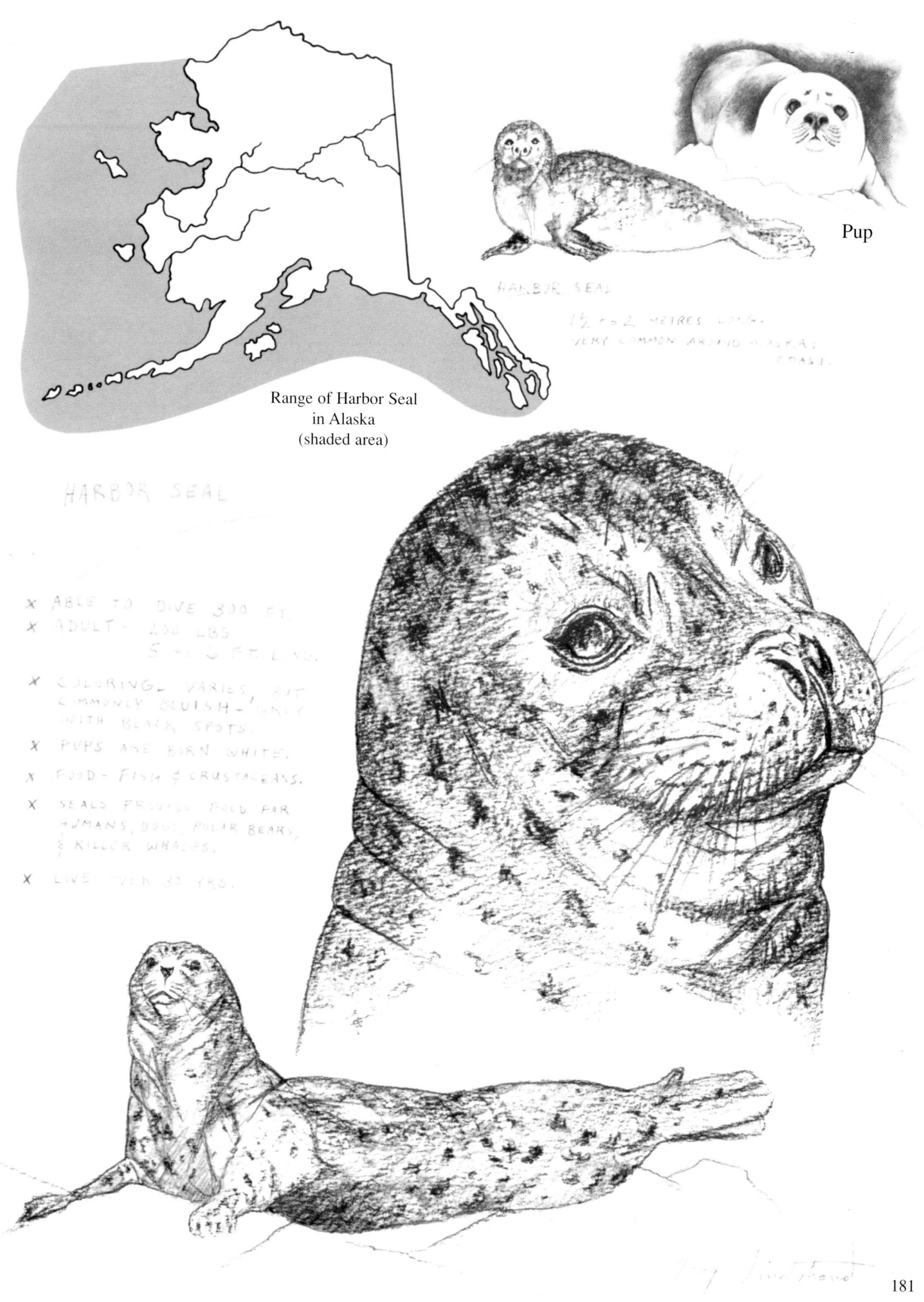

Range of Harbor Seal in Alaska (shaded area)

Pup

Fur Seals

HARP SEAL

1½ to 2 metres long.

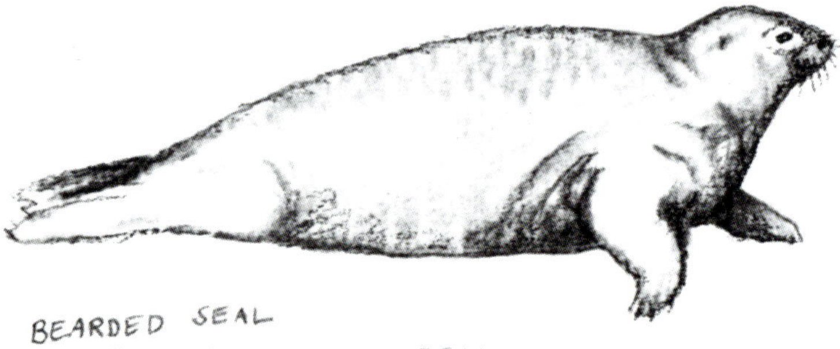

BEARDED SEAL
Alaska's largest seal.
2½ to 3 metres — 500-800 lbs.
Tawny brown to dark brown.
Pups weigh 75 lbs. at birth.

Residents of western coastal villages depend on "oograk" and other seals for a large part of their food. Hides are used to make boat covers, boots, rawhide line, etc.

RIBBON SEAL

1½ to 2 metres long.
Found almost entirely on sea ice.

182

Marten

Ermine

WHITE WHISKERS

Land Otter

LAND OTTER (RIVER)

Sea Otter

183

the PORCUPINE in Alaska

Alaska Department of Fish and Game
Wildlife Notebook Series

The **PORCUPINE** (*Erethizon dorsatum*) is second in size only to the beaver among rodents of Alaska and has the northermnost range of all the world's porcupines. There are few fossil remains of the porcupine and its immediate ancestors, but evidence indicates that they have been a part of the North American fauna since three million years ago when they immigrated north from South America. The porcupine is found throughout all of Alaska except the Alaska Peninsula and Kodiak, Nunivak, and St. Lawrence islands.

GENERAL DESCRIPTION: This stout, short-legged mammal is 25 to 31 inches (73-78 cm) long and is covered with hair and quills of varying length, except on the foot pads and nose. The tips of the long guard hairs are lighter and give coat hues of yellow or white. The hair on the belly is sparse and varies from black to brown. The hair and a thick layer of body fat keep the porcupine warm during the winter. The tail is club-like and the upper surface is heavily covered with quills. The quilled pelage of the porcupine makes it unique among mammals in Alaska. The quills are modified hairs which have microscopic barbs on the tips and are filled with a spongy matrix. Quills from different parts of the body vary in length, flexibility, color, shaft diameter, and barb length.

The average weight of an adult male porcupine ranges from 15 to 18 pounds (7-8.5 kg), but some individuals can weigh up to 25 pounds (11.4 kg). Adult females weigh about 2 pounds less than the males.

The porcupine has excellent senses of smell, hearing, and taste, but its eyesight is poor. Porcupines make a wide variety of sounds ranging from whimpers to screams, depending upon the circumstance.

LIFE HISTORY: Breeding takes place in the fall months from September to November. Males seeking receptive females expand their home ranges up to five times the normal size. If more than one male shows interest in the same female, they will fight for the opportunity to mate with the female. Males use their incisor teeth and quills when fighting, and usually it is the largest and heaviest male which wins dominance. The breeding male then splashes the female with urine. If she is not ready to mate, she shakes off the urine and leaves. If she is ready, she stays and the male mounts in the traditional posture with the female in front and the male in the rear. She will curl her tail over her back, covering most of the quills. Males reach sexual maturity at 24 months and females at 12 months.

After a gestation period of about 210 days, only a single young is born. The gestation period is extremely long for a rodent, twice the time for a beaver. At birth the young weighs between 1 and 2 pounds (0.5-1.0 kg) and is about 10 inches (25 cm) long. Its eyes are open and its body covered with long grayish-black hairs and quills. Within a matter of hours the quills dry and serve as protection. The young porcupine is then capable of following its mother, although the young will not be able to climb large trees for several weeks. The young are able to eat some vegetation after a few weeks, but the female continues nursing the young for 3 1/2 months. During the summer the young stay close to their mothers, learning about den sites and food trees, but toward the end of summer they start to spend more time apart. By October, when the female mates again, the young are fully weaned and wander off to survive the winter alone.

Female porcupines are territorial and will exclude other females, but males will overlap their home ranges. Females have approximately the same size territories, but male home ranges vary according to age and dominance, with the largest. males having the largest ranges.

During the winter, porcupines roost in their dens throughout the day and during periods of cold weather. They use earth or rock caves, hollow logs and trees, or even the thicker vegetation in a tree for dens. In areas without snowfall, dens are not used so much. Porcupines stay active throughout the winter. They feed during the night and during warmer weather.

Porcupines are mainly nocturnal, although they can occasionally be seen during the day Since they roost and feed in trees, one would imagine that they are accomplished tree climbers, but when observed they are slow and awkward. Thirty percent of the animals examined in one study showed evidence of healed fractures indicating that they had fallen out of trees. When climbing the porcupine uses the stiff bristles on the undersurface of the tail as support. The animal has long, curved front claws, which also aid in climbing.

FOOD: The inner bark (phloem and cambium layers) of spruce and hemlock are the major winter foods for porcupine living in Alaska. In the spring and summer, buds and young green leaves of birch, aspen, and willow are eaten until the tannin levels build too high for the porcupine to tolerate. Because they are vegetarians and most vegetable matter is very low in sodium, porcupines need additional sodium in the blood to balance cell potassium levels. As a result, porcupines seek out salt sources such as natural licks, glue which bonds plywood together, human perspiration on tools, road salt, and some paints. Porcupines also feed on shed antlers and the bones of dead animals to obtain sodium.

PREDATION AND DEFENSE: Most carnivores would not pass up a meal of porcupine. However, an encounter between a young inexperienced predator. and a porcupine can be a very painful experience. Some unfortunate carnivores have starved to death because a mouthful of quills has prevented them from eating. In an effort to remove the quills, the predator can cause the barbed quills to work into the deep tissues. However, the quills are coated with a natural antibiotic and rarely cause infection. Predators have different means of killing and eating porcupines. The fisher (not found in Alaska) circles around the porcupine until it can bite its nose. After repeated bites to the nose, the fisher then flips the porcupine over to attack the quill-free belly The porcupine is then eaten, leaving an empty quill-covered skin. This method may also be practiced by lynx, wolves, coyotes, and wolverines, which in Alaska have been recorded eating porcupines.

When the porcupine is relaxed, the hair and quills lie flat and point backwards. When threatened, the porcupine draws up the skin of the back to expose quills facing all directions, and it then presents its formidable bristling back. The porcupine tries to keep its back facing the attacker and strikes back and forth with its tail. Although a porcupine cannot throw its quills, the quills are readily dislodged when the tail is shaken. This may give the impression that quills are being thrown. Recently acquired quills can be easily pulled out of animals with a pair of pliers. If a large number of quills are present. or they have been allowed to work in, the animal will have to be anesthetized in order to remove them.

CONSERVATION AND MANAGEMENT: The porcupine can be easily approached and killed with a club because of its plodding gait. This trait has saved the lives of hungry Natives, trappers, and miners in times past. For this reason, although the hunting season is open all year with no bag limit, many people do not kill porcupines without cause. Some people find the meat too strong, but in some areas of the state, porcupines with their heavy layer of fat are considered a delicacy

Quills sewn onto deerskin used to be the trading wampum of the Northeastern Indian tribes. Quills are still used for decoration by the Athabaskans of Interior Alaska. Natives used to kill porcupines just for their quills, but today the Natives corner the animal and then tap the back of the animal with a styrofoam paddle to collect all the quills they need. The quills are dyed with locally obtainable vegetable materials and then sewn into skin clothing, earrings, and artistic items.

Porcupines can be injurious to commercial forests and reforestation projects by feeding on the terminal buds or eating the bark all the way around the trees. When such problems occur, site specific control may be necessary, although within most of Alaska porcupines are not numerous enough to do much damage.

**"This information was excerpted from the Alaska Department of Fish and Game's Wildlife Notebook Series. For a copy of the complete series, call 907-465-4190 or write ADF&G, Division of Wildlife, P.O. Box 25526, Juneau, Alaska 99811".

Text: Dennis Bromley
Updated and revised by Tim Osborne
Reprinted 1994

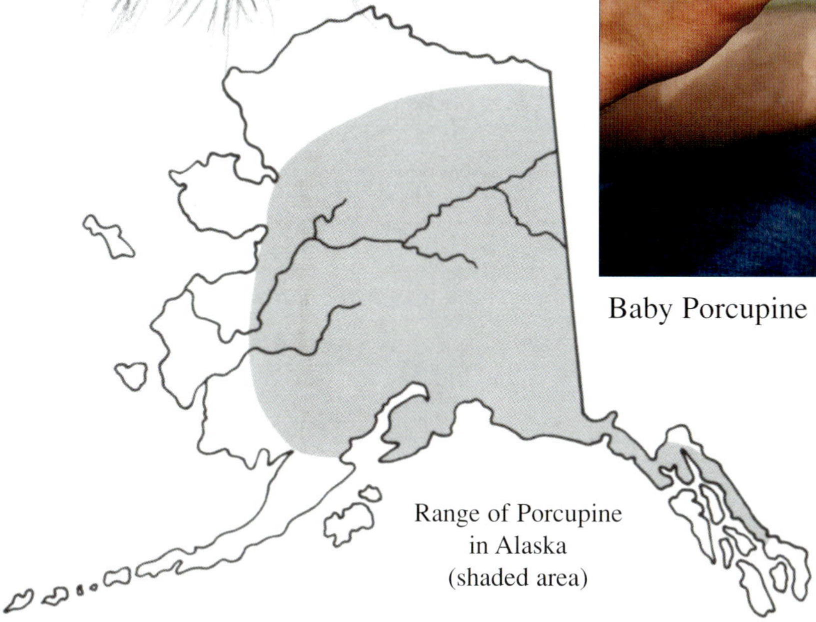

Baby Porcupine (Bottle-fed after mother was killed on highway.)

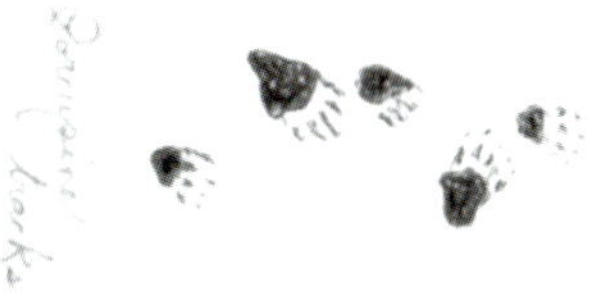

Range of Porcupine in Alaska (shaded area)

Adult

185

the HARE in Alaska

Alaska Department of Fish and Game
Wildlife Notebook Series

There are two species of hares in Alaska, both of which turn white in the winter. **THE SNOWSHOE**, or varying hare (*Lepus americanus*), is the most common and widespread of these. It is distributed over the state except for the lower Kuskokwim Delta, the Alaska Peninsula, and the area north of the Brooks Range. It is sparsely distributed along the southeastern mainland except for major river deltas. **THE ARCTIC HARE** (*Lepus timidus*), also called the tundra or Alaskan hare, populates much of the western coast of Alaska including the Alaska Peninsula but has a spotty distribution along the Arctic coast and the North Slope of the Brooks Range.

Hares are often called rabbits, and both are members of the family Leporidae. However, hares are born fully furred and with eyes open, while newborn rabbits are blind and hairless. Newborn hares are soon able to hop around and leave the nest, but the helpless baby rabbits do not even open their eyes for 7 to 10 days.

GENERAL DESCRIPTION: Snowshoe hares are somewhat larger than cottontail rabbits (*Sylvilagus* spp.). They average around 18 to 20 inches in total length and weigh 3 to 4 pounds. In summer the coat is yellowish to grayish brown with white underparts, and the tail is brown on top. This coat is shed and replaced by white pelage in winter, but the hairs are dusky at the base and the underfur is gray. The ears are dark at the tips. The large hind feet are well-furred, adapting these animals for the very deep snows of the boreal forests—hence the name "snowshoe."

The arctic hare is larger—22 to 28 inches in length and 6 to 12 pounds in weight. The winter coat of this large hare is long, and the fur is white to the base. Edges of the ears are blackish. In summer the coat is grayish brown above and white below, with a whitish base to the hairs. The tail is entirely white.

LIFE HISTORY: Snowshoe hares breed at about 1 year of age and have two to three litters per year. The gestation period is 36 to 37 days. First litters are born around the middle of May in Interior Alaska and average about four leverets (young hares). The second litter in years of increasing abundance often averages six young, and occasionally there is a third litter. Females breed immediately after the birth of a litter.

The leverets are born in an unlined depression or "form." They weigh about 2 ounces at birth and can walk by the time their fur is dry. In a day or two they are wandering about the nest and in less than two weeks will be eating green vegetation. They nurse for about a month. The color pattern of the young snowshoe is similar to the summer pattern of adults.

Breeding habits of the arctic hare are similar, but the reproductive season usually begins later, and there is probably only one litter per year. The leverets are darker than the adults, with a black tinge to their fur.

HABITS: Snowshoe hares are found in mixed spruce forests, wooded swamps, and brushy areas. They feed on a wide variety of plant material—grasses, buds, twigs, and leaves in the summer, and spruce twigs and needles, bark, and buds of hardwood such as aspen and willow in the winter. The arctic hare is generally found on windswept, rocky slopes and upland tundra, often in groups. These big hares usually avoid lowlands and wooded areas. They feed on willow shoots and various dwarf arctic plants.

Hares are most active at dusk and dawn. They do not dig burrows or build nests but use natural shelters and depressions and rest under branches or bushes. The snowshoe hare travels about on well-established trails or runways, which become deeply worn in the snow or forest floor. It is interesting that the winter trails through the deep snow follow the summer pathways.

Populations of snowshoe hares are subject to cycles of high abundance and scarcity. The population in an area will build up over a period of years to a peak of abundance, followed by a sudden decline to a very low level. During periods of peak abundance, there are as many as 600 animals per square mile of range. The exact cause or causes of the decline are unknown. Some possibilities include overbrowsing their food supply, predators, shock disease due to stress, parasites, or a combination of these.

ECONOMIC IMPORTANCE: Snowshoe hares are one of the more important food items of northern furbearers, particularly lynx. They are often an important source of food for Alaskans. The arctic hare is also important as a source of food and fur.

In times of great abundance, the snowshoes may kill brush by overbrowsing. In "high" years they may compete with big game animals such as moose for forage.

Both species of hare offer a great deal of recreation for the small game hunter, especially in years of abundance. The arctic hare provides an unusual trophy and a considerable amount of meat. The snowshoe is available to more hunters and can be taken near highway systems and in such disturbed areas as mine tailing piles. Hares are best hunted with a shotgun and birdshot, .22-caliber rifle, or handgun. Early snowfalls will often catch the snowshoe hare still in its summer coat, making it vulnerable to the hunter. The meat is quite tasty.

Hunters should be alert for signs of tularemia, a bacterial disease found in hares and rodents throughout the world. Such signs include general sluggishness and spots on the liver and spleen. Normal sanitary precautions should be taken when handling hares, and rubber gloves should be used when cleaning and dressing them. The meat should be cooked thoroughly.

Text: Jeannett R. Earnest
Revised 1989. Reprinted 1994

Lynx

Snowshoe Hare

Hare tracks

Summer Coat

Large feet help to propel it across snow.

Range of Arctic and Snowshoe Hares in Alaska

Arctic Hare
Snowshoe Hare

Snowshoe Hare / Winter coat

Beaver Study

Adult Beaver

Alaska Department of Fish and Game
Wildlife Notebook Series

Red Squirrel

The **RED SQUIRREL** (Tamiasciurus hudsonicus) makes itself quite conspicuous with its lively habits and noisy chatter. Cone cuttings on stumps or rocks are common, and tracks in snow are numerous where this squirrel occurs. It can be found in spruce forests over most of Alaska and has a wide range in North America. It occupies a wide variety of forest habitat, occurring in the hardwood forests of eastern North America and the coniferous forests of the west and north.

GENERAL DESCRIPTION: The active rodent averages 11 to 13 inches in length (28-33 cm), including tail, and is a rusty-olive color on the upper parts of its body with a whitish belly and underparts. In summer, a dark stripe on the side separates the upper rusty color from the white of the belly. The bushy tail is often a lighter orange or red with light tipped hairs.

LIFE HISTORY: Red squirrels are solitary but pair for mating in February and March. Females usually breed when they are 1 year old. Three to seven young are born after a gestation period of 36 to 40 days. The young are born blind and hairless, weighing about 1/4 ounce at birth. They are weaned at about 5 weeks but remain with the female until almost adult size.

The young leave the female and are independent during their first winter. This means that they have to be successful at gathering and storing a winter's supply of food.

Arctic Ground Squirrel

Hoary Marmot

Hoary Marmot

Arctic Ground Squirrel

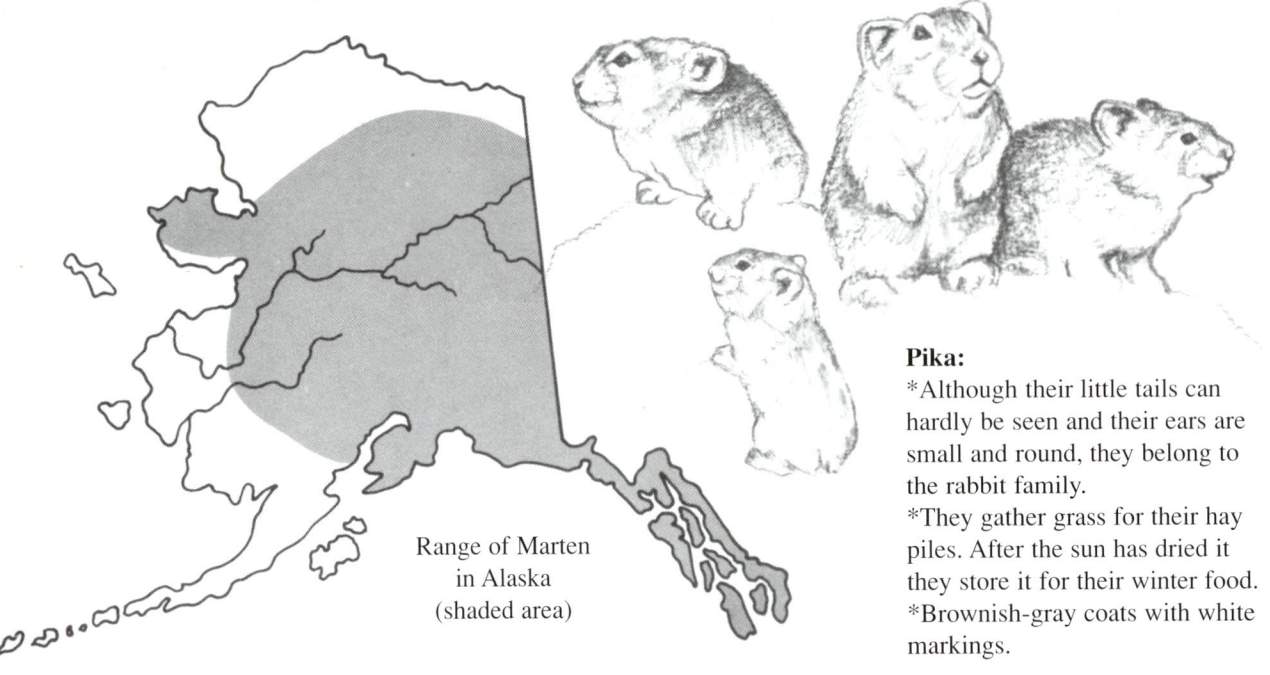

Range of Marten in Alaska (shaded area)

Pika:
*Although their little tails can hardly be seen and their ears are small and round, they belong to the rabbit family.
*They gather grass for their hay piles. After the sun has dried it they store it for their winter food.
*Brownish-gray coats with white markings.

Pika

Short-tailed Weasel (winter coat)

Marten

Marten: Martens are very inquisitive and can often be coaxed to come near by making mouse-like squeaks. Looks a lot like a weasel. Weight: 2 - 3 1/2 #'s
Weasel: Coats are brown and white in summer and entirely white (except for black-tipped tail) during the winter. Mice, shrews and voles are their primary prey.

Short-tailed Weasel (Ermine) / summer coat.

Alaska photographer Calvin Hall canoes in the scenic Turnagain Arm area.

Orcas ("killer" whales) patrol Resurrection Bay near Seward, Alaska.

A *good day* of halibut fishing! / July, 2005 / Ninilchik, Alaska

Tour boats out of Seward, Alaska often see whales as they migrate to their summer feeding-grounds here in Alaska. Humpback whales, like the one shown, generally follow coastlines and take advantage of seasonal currents during their travels. In the autumn, the whales head south to winter in the tropical waters of Hawaii; in spring they return to their northern feeding grounds for the summer months.

The majestic and acrobatic Humpback whales can throw themselves completely out of the water when breaching. Other feats include lifting their large flukes out of the water and slapping them down on the surface (called tail-lobbing) and also slapping the water with their long flippers (called flipper-slapping).

Threats to the protected species include: depletion of the whale's prey species, becoming entangled in commercial fishing nets, and the potential risk posed by oil spills.

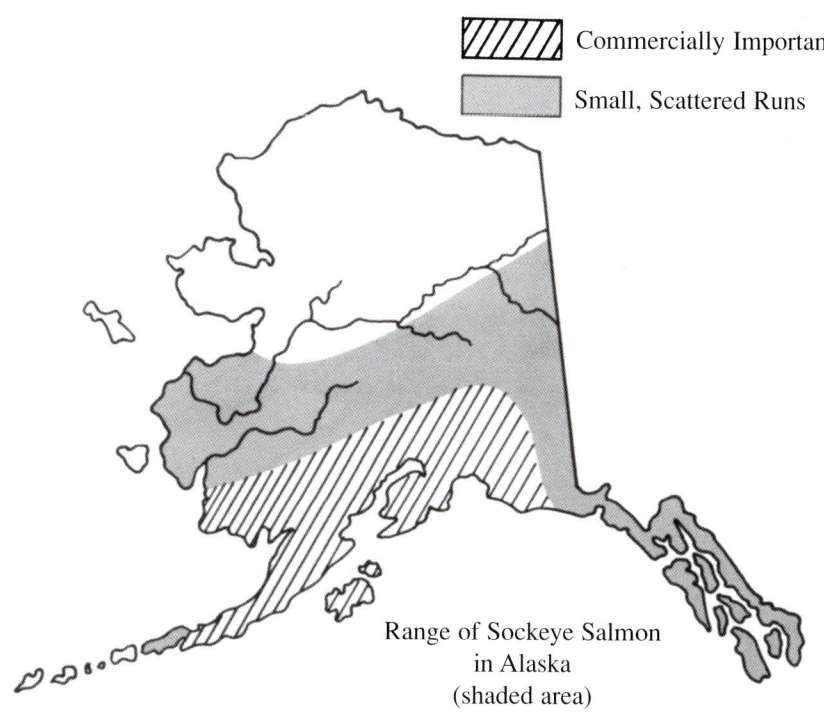

Range of Sockeye Salmon
in Alaska
(shaded area)

Red Salmon (spawning)

August Lindstrand (Dad) returning from successful halibut charter. His biggest was 115 pounds.

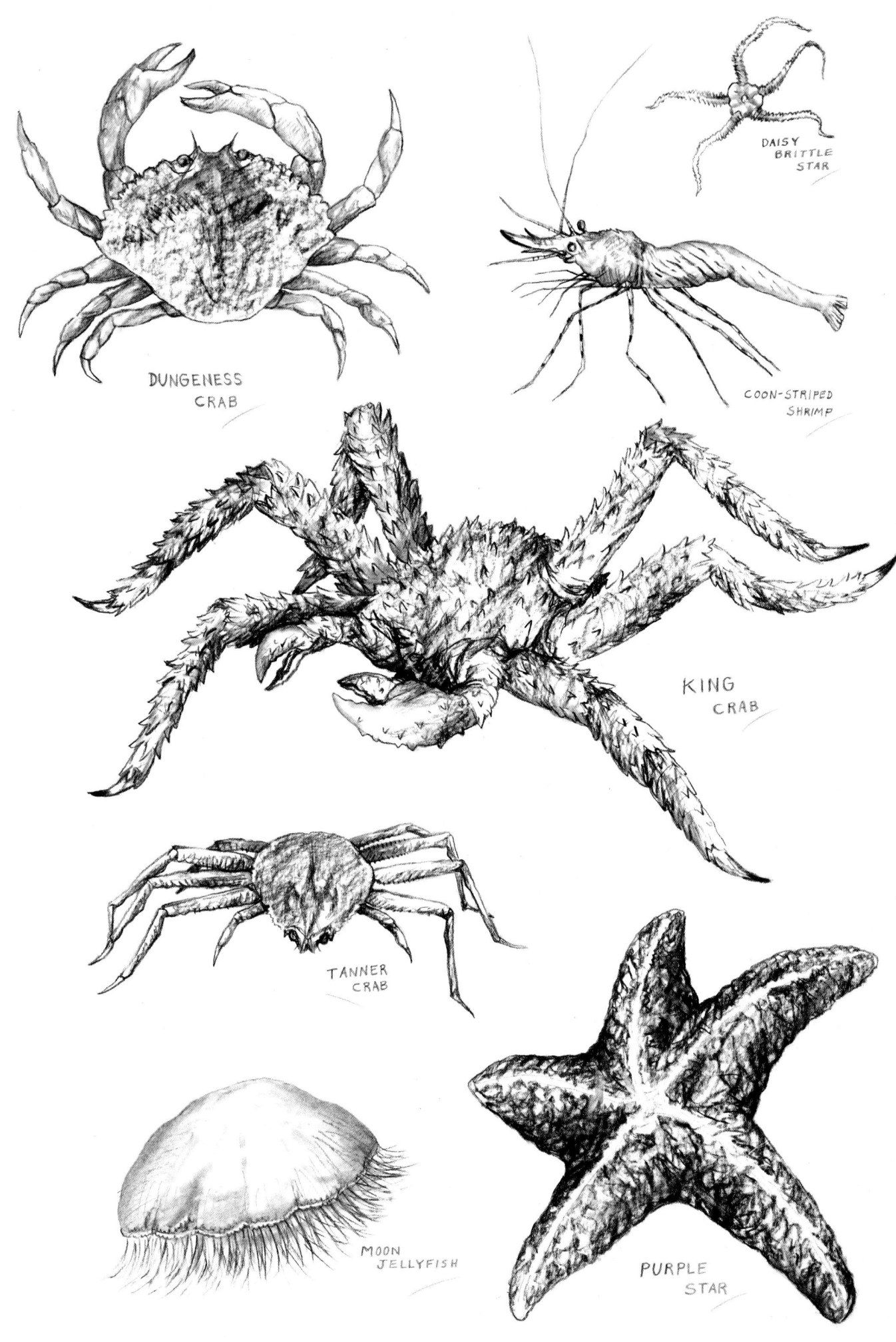

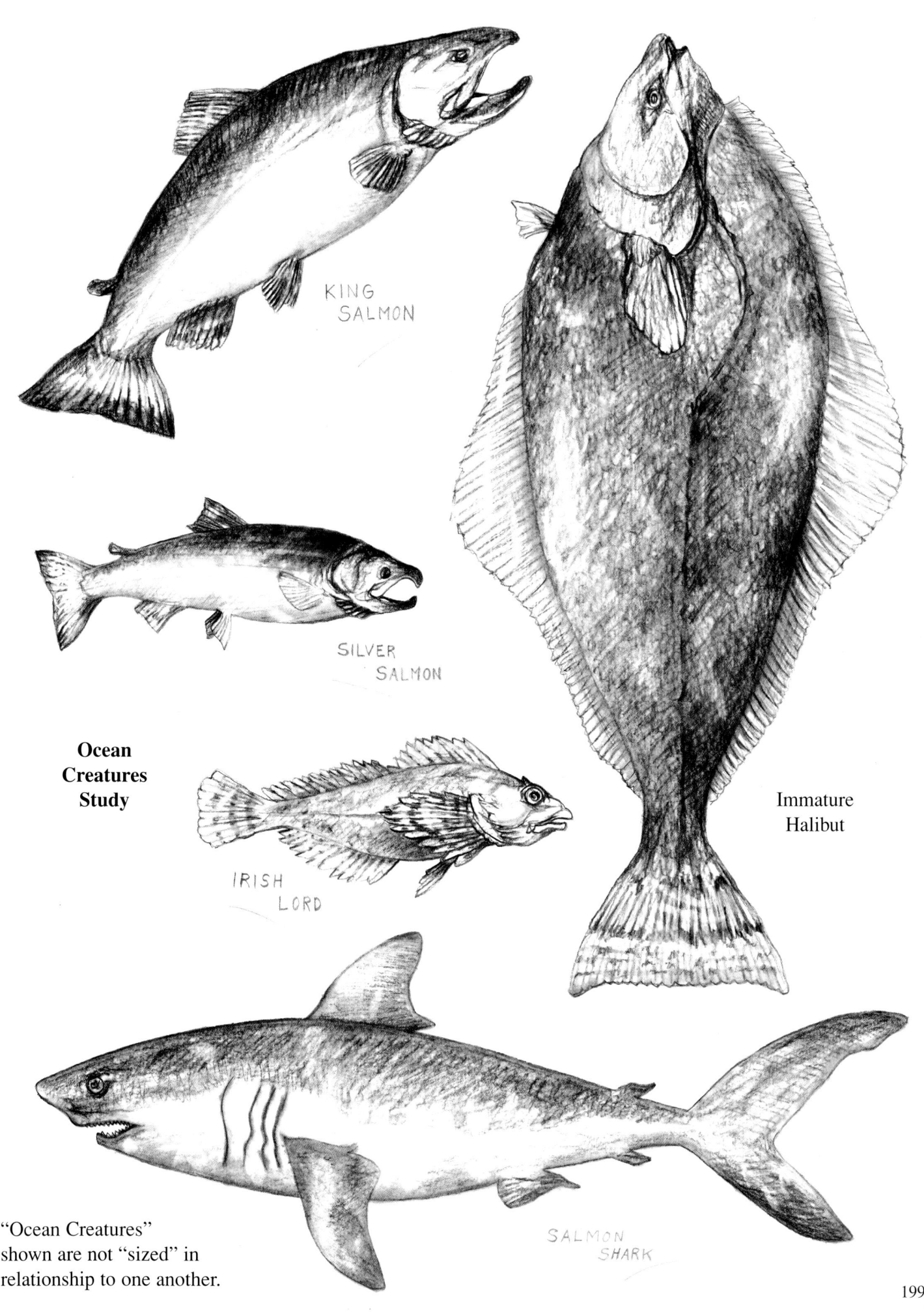

JOURNAL

Throughout my Alaskan travels I have tried to keep a daily journal; jotting down the happenings of the day, my thoughts and observations. To share years and years of daily notes is not only outside the scope of this Sketchbook, but would, I fear, bore most. I thought, however, that by picking out a few of the *choicer* daily jottings may be of some interest to some.

The selected record that follows is not a fully complete record; that is, I have tried to cull out all of my *personal* life and record only that which I felt applied to my life as a lover of nature, artist and photographer and what I saw through the eyes of a person in this pursuit.

Left Minnesota on June 10th, 1970, having ended my commercial art job a few days prior and having traded my Corvette convertible for a 4-WD Ford Bronco. Miles passed, days, a week, and soon the gravel roads of Canada gave way to pavement. Alaska. After crossing the border I almost immediately saw three moose trotting across a hillside. Alaska was surely the *promised land* I thought, equal to the rampant wild imaginings of my mind.

WARNING: This journal was not professionally edited and was typeset as my *scribbled* notes read. Therefore, the grammatical errors are mine alone. Since this "Sketchbook" is a very "personal thing" (a one-man's effort) I felt that I'd rather have my notes recorded as I had written them than of having them rewritten, improved and corrected by someone else. *I'm sure I'll probably get flak on this decision!*

So then, my Alaska journal.

---

24 June, 1970 (Cantwell area)

Hiked around the area the past few days. Not much going on here as it is a very small town. However, some nice, friendly and helpful people here. Have been camping on the outskirts of town. Did get some OK Hawk owl and ptarmigan photos and finished a few bird sketches which I'll try to sell.

Over my campfire tonight I thought: *"Wow, I am actually here in Alaska!"* I still remember my first glimpse of Alaska; I remember looking out of the window of a military airliner and seeing a small cabin on the edge of a remote lake with a thin, straight column of chimney smoke rising above it. And I remember thinking of it as I spent a year in the jungles of Vietnam and later while finishing college in Minnesota. I promised myself that I would someday come here and spend a winter in a remote cabin such as that. And now, here I finally am in America's "Last Frontier".☺

Hawk Owl

26 June, 1970 (Fairbanks area)

Arrived in Fairbanks late yesterday morning. I get the impression that I got here a hundred years too late. It certainly seems more "cosmopolitan" than I had imagined it would be. A certain *frontier* flavor, true, but also a tinge of that old Minneapolis "civilization".

The sun never seems to set this far north during this time of year and people seem as apt to be up and about at 2 A.M. as 2 P.M.

Incidentally, every other establishment downtown seems to be a saloon. An old-fashioned saloon brawl erupted in one on Second Ave. As I quietly sat there perched on a stool, everything, including nearby barstools and an elderly Eskimo gent went a'flying through the smoke-filled air.

This looked to be exciting country hereabouts. I think tonight I shall toast my arrival.

5 July, 1970 (Mt. McKinley Nat'l Park)

My birthday. Spent the day (and yesterday) up amongst a few bands of Dall sheep; ewes with lambs and also a band of four rams. A *fitting* way to start off one's 27th year, hey?

A few Golden eagles soared effortlessly on outstretched wings in the high mountain currents. Watched the playful lambs kicking up their heels across crags and lush green meadows. A family of fox kits curled up outside their den in the foothills and snoozed in the warm afternoon sun.

What *more* could one possibly want for birthday presents?

Dall Rams

26 July, 1970

Back in "Denali" to photograph and sketch. Today I saw twelve grizzlies. Smokes!

A Ranger told me that there are an estimated 70 *grizzlies* in this National Park; probably the greatest concentrations of grizzlies left in the world. He also informed me that Brown bears and grizzlies are really the same specie. However, biologists distinguish them by calling the bears that are "inland" *grizzlies* and those that are "coastal" are called *Brown bears*. This specie, of course, is different from the Black bear and Polar bear species.

He also told me that Mount McKinley National Park was formed primarily for the caribou herds, but that during the winter the caribou migrate outside the north Park boundary and are there susceptible to hunting. Also, since the Park's wolves follow the caribou herds, they too are hunted, trapped and poached.

Incidentally, everyone I talk to hereabouts seems to either *love* the wolf or *hate* the wolf. Few are undecided.

30 July, 1970

Followed a small pack of wolves around most of the day. Last night I heard wolves (probably the same pack) howling from out across the Toklat river flats. So beautiful that sound; yet so chilling and eerie. It's truly the whole romance of the wilderness balled up and condensed into this one sound. All the mystique and wonder of the Far North condensed into that mournful, quavering cry.

Early this morning I glassed the area in back of the river flats and soon focused on some dark spots well over a mile away. Wolves. I packed up my backpack and crossed over into the area, having to cross several shallow icy-cold glacier streams on the way.

I followed them for a few hours, trying to keep pace. Whenever I would try to pick up my pace and close the gap, they too would speed up. I was, seemingly, as close as they wished me. They knew I was here and they accepted me...to a degree. Less than a hundred yards did not seem to fall within that *degree*.

I did learn that the wolf certainly hunts other things besides moose and caribou (reportedly their main food source). The pack flushed a covey of young ptarmigan from a brushy area and one wolf jumped high and actually appeared to snatch one fluttering bird out of the air. An unbelievable feat of timing and agility! Another bird was apparently run down by another wolf, for it too laid down to eat something.

Sure wish I could've gotten' closer.

3 August, 1970 (Anchorage)

Arrived in Anchorage last night. Came primarily to get myself a dog. After arriving at the dog pound this morning and browsing through the strays and drop-offs I came on one that struck my fancy. It was named Chinook and it was dropped off for being too aggressive. A male, 4 months old, and a quarter-wolf.

I had found my dog.

7 August, 1970 (Hope area)

Am hiking the Resurrection Trail. Guess it's 30 some miles. Have seen 4 moose and 7 Black bears the past two days. All, with the exception of one Black bear, have been seen as I sat on some tree stump or hillside and glassed the valleys and other hillsides. This one *exception* happened about mid-morning today.

Chinook was somewhere in back of me, sniffing and snooping around in every bush and deadfall we passed. I didn't pay him any mind, as whenever he'd lose sight of me he'd come hell-bent down the trail until he caught up. I had just begun climbing out of the bottom of a ridge and was about half-way UP the slope when a large Black bear came around a corner heading DOWN the slope. His nose was dragging the ground as though following a scent.

"Hey!" I yelled, "HEY, HEY, HEY!" I had a rifle along, so slipped it off from around my neck and chambered a round. Naturally, all this took about twenty times longer than it now takes to tell about it, what with the sling snagging snugly on the frame of the backpack and all! Well, as soon as I was ready to *protect myself* if he decided to charge, he had already turned tail and fled like a fat, black jellybean; spraying digested poop out for the first 10 yards.

A moment later Chinook showed up to see what all the darn ruckus was about. As soon as he caught a whiff of "bar", his hair all stood up and he finally acted *serious* for a brief moment. He even did a little growl.

Ten minutes later, however, he was back chasing his tail and pouncing on pinecones. The bear incident was evidently long forgotten.

This was the dog I had chosen to protect me? Lord, have mercy……

14 Sept., 1970 (Paradise Lake; an hours flight out of Moose Pass)

Flew out of Moose Pass early this morning. Destination: Paradise Lake. The pilot, Wayne Racine, told me it was one of his favorite fishing lakes.

Took me a few hours to set up a good camp; a sleeping tent, a ten foot square of Visqueen (to cook under) and a good, safe fire pit. This would be my home for the next ten days.

Chinook At Camp

17 Sept., 1970

Last night I again drifted off to sleep to the cry of some loons. "Ooo-luu-lee," they mourn. "Ooo-luu-lee". It is a sound known by those of us who hike the shorelines of wild lakes and who have camped near moonlit trout waters and stoked crackling campfires. It is a *true* wilderness sound.

Weather has been good so far. My lips are parched from the sun and the wind. My face has certainly never been browner. Am averaging *more* than one grayling or rainbow trout on every two/three casts. That ain't *bad fishing* my friend!

Chinook went nosing around earlier and brought home a few porcupine quills in his nose to show for it. I wrestled him into my sleeping bag and managed to hold his mouth shut while pulling the quills with my fishing pliers. By finishing time I wasn't exactly Chinook's best friend! Later I won his friendship back by frying him up a big plate of fish, Friskies and beef broth.

1 Oct., 1970 (Healy area)

His golden red coat glistening in the morning's sun, the fox pranced gracefully along his chosen game trail; his small, black-capped feet touching as lightly as a fallen feather. He pauses, listening for the faintest rustle of grass to disclose where a meal hides. Or, he creeps and slinks until his prey is within reach, then leaps out of hiding and finishes it off with a quick bite.

This then is the hunting method of the Red fox I watched and followed off and on during the day. Wary, sharp-witted, and a true athlete. The shrews and mice were definitely outclassed!

15 Oct., 1970 (Birch Lake)

Spent the day duck hunting out of a blind on the southwest edge of the lake. Bagged a few; enough for a couple meals.

Perhaps I'd best back up. I've rented a cabin out near Birch Lake, 50-some miles south of Fairbanks, for the winter. No electricity but at least I think I can swing the $50 monthly rent and still have a few bucks left over for painting supplies and a little grub. My intention is to hole-up here and paint and draw until Spring.

24 Oct., 1970

Started working Chinook in a harness today. He wasn't too wild about the harness at first and made all sorts of jumps and twists to remove it, but by this afternoon he seemed to settle down a bit and began to accept its inevitability. I started him out by having him pull a little block of wood around the yard. Everytime he heard the block of wood moving behind him he'd flip around and pounce on it.

I hooked a rope to his collar and then walked away some ten feet and called him over. By yanking on the rope every time he tried to twist around he began to understand, and soon he would come running to me with only an occasional glance over his shoulder.

25 Oct., 1970

Spent a few hours with my sled-dog today. The key to success is probably repeat, repeat, repeat. Also, a lot of praise when he does it right.

Chinook followed me around to my rabbit snares today, pulling a little-heavier block of wood all the way. As soon as he gets used to pulling a weight behind him I'll switch him over to a small sled.

Shoeshoe Hare

29 Oct., 1970

Still spending my days at the drawing board spreading either charcoal or paint. These Coleman gas-lanterns certainly aren't the best lights to work under, so I'm trying to set my hours so that I'll have all my early morning chores done by the time it gets light enough to sit down near the window and work. As soon as it starts getting dark again in the afternoon, I put aside my pencils and brushes and go out to check my rabbit snares or go grouse hunting. Then I cook us up some sort of meal and later wash dishes. After that it's time to pump up the lanterns again and, with one hanging over each shoulder, go back to work on my easel or drawing board.

Do see a few neighbors up the road every once in a while but usually I try to stay by myself as much as I can and try to accomplish some artwork. When one is self-employed he really has to discipline himself to do his work. It is, believe me, *very* easy to get distracted and goof-off.

18 Jan., 1971

Saw an amazing thing early today down near the lake. I was snowshoeing around and grouse hunting when (as I was passing a deadfall) a weasel shot out and, like a bullet, hit a snowshoe hare that was crouched a few feet away near some willows it had been feeding on.

Just a flash of white fur hitting another patch of white fur. Around and around the two went, the weasel at times riding the hare's back, biting and slashing. The much larger hare was kicking and jumping trying to dislodge it.

This seemed to take only a few minutes before the hare stopped fighting, gave a long quiver and then was still. The weasel stood next to it with his front paws atop the hare's head. I had watched this unfold from a ringside seat only about twenty feet away. I walked over to them and the weasel ran off, scurried up a nearby slanted tree and sat there looking at me. I picked the hare up and could see that its neck and back of its head were bloody. I tossed the hare over to the base of the weasel's tree. He came down, sniffed it and then climbed up and sat down.

My cabin was about a mile away so I put the gear in "jog" (ever try that with snowshoes on?) and went for my camera. When I finally returned back the weasel had dragged the hare under the deadfall.

Strong little squirt! And camera-shy too.

26 Jan., 1971

We have been having a barrage of Northern Lights filled nights lately. If I'm up late working, I'll often walk outside and watch them for a few minutes before then going to bed.

Read a Robert Service verse on the Northern Lights recently. The Yukon bard said it well, for it is with true "awe" that one watches one of these colorful displays of celestial battles charge across the northern skies. It chills, for it is as if the sky had caught afire and was spitting out sparks across the universe.

Perhaps this is how life on earth will someday end? God will merely light a match to the sky.

28 May, 1971 (*Mt. McKinley Nat'l Park*)

Spent the last two nights up on the slopes and ridges of Polychrome Pass and the East Fork. Caught a bus ride out and left my car back at a lodge outside the Park,

It's great having all this daylight at this time of year. If I wasn't wearing a watch I'd never know what time it actually was! And the animals too, they're as likely to be grazing or browsing at midnight as at noon. Of course there's still only one *dawn* and *sunset*; the times when I get my best "light" for shootin'.

The wild flowers are beginning to make their appearance here on the high slopes. I laid on my belly and studied about 4 different species. I never paid much attention to tiny flowers before, but here, up high in this remote and wild place it seems so natural to stretch out on the ground and *discover* them. Being alone in a wilderness area will often inspire one to pause more to *discover* new treasures and to move in a more leisurely and observant pace. Today, in the *real* world of concrete and materialism, the small mountain flower is often overlooked.

How simple things have now become for me, now that I have left the world of art deadlines and jammed freeways. I now live in a world where there is time to pause, or to (at least) slow one's step so as not to miss a peek at a fragile mountain flower or to listen to the soft "baa-aa-ing" of a newly born lamb while sharing a meadow together.

Small Mountain Flowers / Quarter

1 June, 1971

Been a great few days hereabouts. Lots of wildlife to sketch and photograph. A LOT of bears here this summer!

Earlier this afternoon I sat on a hillside and watched as a Golden eagle swept down out of the sky and killed a marmot that was sunning himself on a rocky ridge, not knowing it was under attack until the moment before the eagle struck it. The marmot had been a bit careless, and here in this savage land of winged predators, it has cost him his life.

I watched this tale unfold through my binoculars. After the marmot lay dead, the eagle threw back its head and seemed to scream a silent scream across the valley, as if to tell the world of its feat. It struck me as a magnificent gesture, *one I shan't ever forget*.

Here were two wild creatures that lived because they were wary and they were healthy and hardy. They lived by their wits, every moment important, because the difference between living or dieing is often dealt out without so much as a split-moments notice. Carelessness has cost one of nature's children its life, but with the giving of this life, another creature was assured of life for a while longer. Today the marmot, or prey, has perished; tomorrow the eagle, or predator, may perish because its prey had proven too wary or was too scarce to feed him and his predator brothers.

It was the way of *predator and prey*. And today, up here in the high-country, it was all explained seemingly *just for me*.

Marmot

25 Aug., 1971 (*Circle City. A few miles s. of the Arctic Circle*)

Hitched a ride with a trapper about 20 miles up the Yukon River yesterday. We almost ended up in trouble when his beautiful dog (who was tied in the boat) chewed through the rope that we had tied the boat to a tree with. Luckily this took place at another trapper's cabin (Jim and Kathy) so when we saw that our boat was gone we were able to run it down and recover it with their boat.

The boat was a mile downstream when we overtook it; spinning and bobbing in the churning Yukon currents like a hunk of driftwood afloat.

I had a couple of cameras and lenses in a packsack in the front of the boat and the packsack was wet. The boat must've taken a few bad waves. Had I lost these cameras I fear I may have had to *get a job* (perish the thought!) in order to replace them. Also, had the boat swamped, the tied dog surely would've gone down, and there's no replacing a good friend. And to a bachelor trapper like "Trapper", this dog was his only companion and quite likely his best and truest friend.

After recovering the boat and lunching on hot cinnamon rolls back at the cabin, we headed back downriver.

We pulled up on the beach upriver from Circle that night. The case of beer that Trapper had bought earlier had rapidly *evaporated* on us and Trapper beached us at such a speed that it was unnecessary to pull the boat further up on the beach, as the boat was snugly jammed up between two bushes.

I ate some Oreos and drank some tea before spreading my sleeping bag under the big Alaskan sky and dozing off. Trapper was nestled in a little clump of bushes snoring up a storm. On a rotted stump beside him sat a half-empty bottle of beer. He certainly lived life in his own chosen way.

27 August, 1971

"Trapper" hauled me back to Circle City this afternoon. I retrieved Chinook from a family there that was kind enough to look after him for awhile. Trapper's male dog and mine were deadly enemies and they would've likely chewed each other up.

His remote cabin is some 60 miles up the Yukon, so this trip will be his last until break-up next spring. He's anxious to get back home and buck up some more wood and to also build some lynx-houses along his trap line. These *houses* are built of sticks and Spruce boughs and he will later set bait and traps inside them. Without the house's protection, the snow would likely cover the traps too much and make them ineffective. Also, he wants to "jerky" up a caribou and net some salmon and sheefish for him and his dog. He also wanted a grizzly.

Trapper, I truly wish you the best.

21 Sept., 1971 (Mankomen Lake)

Landed at Mankomen Lake today. Home for the winter. Cleo McMahan from Gakona flew me, my dog and our gear in, in two trips. Spent the day browsing around and unpacking. I'm definitely excited about this new country and my being able to spend the winter alone here.

Mankomen Lake is about 40 miles east of Paxson, Alaska, and to my knowledge my nearest neighbor is probably about 35 miles away (as the crow flies). The lake is about 3 miles long and probably 3/4's of a mile wide. It sits in a little bowl with mountains all around. The land hereabouts is tundra and spruce-studded. I would judge it to be prime game country.

Earlier tonight three moose were feeding on the water plants in the bay across the lake from the cabin.

Goodnight world, I'm bushed…

Mankomen Lake Cabin

6 Oct., 1971

Company last night. Univited! Three grizzlies.

Chinook woke me at about midnight (I'd guess) and when I looked out the front window I saw three huge hulks pass by (their tracks were later found to be only four steps from the front door). I grabbed my rifle and chambered a round, thinking for sure they were coming in for supper….and that *supper* was me!

Instead, they walked around the edge of the cabin and headed for the meat shed where some moose quarters were hanging. The moon was out and bright and I watched these three bears try to claw their way through to the meat. They would seemingly change off, each one having a try at the closed door. I watched them with a big flashlight until I felt they were getting too close to figuring out how to get the door open. I then went through the unheated storage room and leaned out of the backdoor. They saw and heard me instantly and turned to face me. When the flashlight's beam of light fell on the sow, the one cub swatted at the moving light and struck her fairly hard. At this she gave out a chilling "waw" and took off, the two cubs right behind her. When they started moving, I slammed the back door shut and dropped the crossbar in place, as I wasn't sure *which way* they were going to *move*.

When I got back into the main room I found Chinook barking and clawing through the plastic sheeting I had placed over a few windows to help insulate them. I started to yell at him but instead just told him to cool down, shook my head, added a little wood to the stove and crawled back into bed. I would recover the windows tomorrow if there's enough plastic left.

17 Oct., 1971

Two grizzlies left their tracks in back of the cabin last night. Hope they go into hibernation soon! This is truly some prime grizzly country as I'm always coming across tracks or scat while hiking around the area.

I glassed three caribou swimming across the lake as I stood on the beach at the west end of the lake this afternoon. They beached about a hundred feet west of my cabin, shook, and disappeared into the hills.

Tonight, a beautiful night. No big-city or civilization noises to distract from the sounds and sights of Nature. No sirens or TV to drown out the whisperings of the wind; no glaring lights or tall buildings to rob ones sight of the Northern Lights or of the moon, slowly drifting above snow-smothered mountains. And to breath the crisp, wilderness air is to know you are truly alive. Tonight, God, the feeling of my freedom is a silent conversation between You and I. Here I can view the power of Your hand: the mountains, lake and sky. Here then is my cathedral. Here than my faith is strong and I believe completely. In the city, amongst man and his puny sculptures of concrete, metal and glass, I sometimes lose sight of Your natural wonders. It is then that I sometimes momentarily lose sight of You.

14 November, 1971

Hundreds and hundreds of caribou moving through the area. Very unusual to look out the window and not see dozens of caribou migrating by during these past few days.

Yesterday I shot a young bull down the lake. I dressed the animal before going back home for the rest of my utensils and to harness Chinook up to his sled. Then I skinned the caribou and broke the meat up into three piles, each pile representing a sled load. By about six, in pitch dark, we arrived home with our last load. We were both bushed!

I put the liver in a bowl of salt water to soak overnight. Tomorrow it'll be liver and onions and homemade blueberry jam for the sourdough muffins.

1 December, 1971

Woke up early this morning to find a dog standing with his nose against the window and his front feet on my face. Outside the window stood a fox looking in. What a *different* way to start the day, hey?

I flipped the dog off my bed and let Chinook out; watching the two canines disappear behind the woodshed. I slipped my feet into a pair of Bunny boots and, still in shorts (only!) I ran out, hearing the fight raging atop the hill. A whole lot of flopping around and "yipping" and snarling.

By the time I made my *memorable* dash through the two feet of snow in nothing but foot-high boots and a pair of Fruit-Of-The-Loom shorts, Chinook had the fox by the neck and pinned to the ground while the fox had a mouthful of Chinook's neck fur. After a few minutes of my moving closer and yelling and whooping, the two broke apart and I rolled the fox with my .22.

I grabbed the fox by the tail and made a mad dash back to the house; yelling and acting as only one who is totally alone and forty miles from his nearest neighbor could possibly act! Dropping the fox at the door, kicking off unlaced boots, I dove for the bed and burrowed back down into the quilts until the pain of the cold subsided.

Surely the rest of the day will be hopelessly *dull* when compared to this morning's *wild beginning*.

Red Fox / "Cross" Color Phase

9 December, 1971

Almost think that I was visited by some thieves this morning. I had slept in and the fire had long since gone out. Then I heard a plane buzz the cabin and I hopped up and got dressed. When I went outside a few minutes later the plane was just about to sit down on the lake ice in front of the cabin. I walked out towards the dock and, just as the plane's skis hit the ice, the pilot poured the coals back on and went tearing on by me and lifted into the sky. I watched it continue on down the valley and through the pass.

Of course I didn't comprehend all this at first, but later when I got to thinking, it all added up to that: a thief on wings, flying into remote bush cabins and robbing them of their guns and the multitude of other things needed to stock a bush cabin.

Sure wish I could've been more alert and noticed the plane's number. The plane was a small tail-dragger, white with red markings. That's all I saw before it disappeared in a flurry of blown snow.

Scum of the North.

20 December, 1971

-54 degrees today. Rather nippy. Not, however, as dramatic as Jack London (or others?) inferred in his Northland novels. One's breath does not freeze as soon as it hits the air and spit does not freeze solid before it hits the ground.

Another common assumption of -50 degree weather is that animals all hole up and don't move. Today I saw a wolverine cross the east end of the lake and three wolves patrolling the south edge. Perhaps some *hole up* but most predators can ill afford such nonsense as that.

But, I don't think I'll chop wood today. Wimp! Instead we'll just hang out *indoors*. ☺

26 December, 1971

Seeing a number of wolves lately. A pair of dark-colored ones crossed through the middle of the lake earlier today. Should probably set some traps and bait them with a kept moose and caribou head. Will also not let Chinook roam far away as wolves love to eat dogs!

Running low on vegetables, etc. My pilot Cleo usually flies in once a month and brings me prearranged supplies and also my mail. I usually keep a pot of caribou or moose stew on the stove and I noticed that I'm out of carrots and onions. Cleo usually comes about this time of month but bad weather can sometimes delays his flights. He is a well respected pilot in these parts and I think he also does some flying for Alaska's Dept. of Fish & Game.

Reminds me of an old Alaskan "saying": "*There are many BOLD pilots up here and many OLD pilots, but no OLD, BOLD pilots!*"

Chinook pulled five loads of wood from the woods. Plan to bring some more in tomorrow as there's a well-packed trail blazed right now and I would like to move in a bunch of wood before it snows again.

10 January, 1972

Four caribou passed the west edge of the lake this morning. A cow and calf moose passed on the frozen lake in front of the cabin yesterday. A big flock of about fifty ptarmigan were also bedded down in the snow there and I just happened to be outside watching when the moose flushed them. That was a pretty sight!

22 January, 1972

Woke up to a cabin full of smoke last night! The lake was having another one of its week-long "blows", and the strong winds together with all the sappy green Spruce logs I'd been burning, clogged the chimney-cap and backed up all the smoke through the stove and into the cabin.

Chinook woke me by barking and whining, and when I opened my eyes I thought the cabin was on fire for sure. I leaped up, grabbed a bucket of water and threw it into the smoking, smoldering stove (don't ask me *why* I did such a thing!) before jumping into some pants and boots and going outside with Chinook.

I could not see anything inside the cabin, as the smoke was *that* thick, and my throwing the pail of water into the smoldering wood just made it smoke all the more.

Finally I woke up enough to realize the cabin was not on fire but that the chimney was clogged and wasn't letting the smoke out.

Freezing, in the dark and in the seemingly -100 degree wind-chilled night, I scrambled atop the cabin and with a fireplace poker was able to open the sap-clogged vents in the chimney-cap. I then went back down and tried to revive my swamped fire and also trying to herd the smoke out've the cabin by swinging a bath towel around. It was 2:30 A.M. and I knew I wouldn't be able to go back to sleep again. I put on the teapot and huddled in my parka and blankets until the smoke finally cleared and the fire revived.

Not sure if breathing smoke can eventually kill you but I definitely think my buddy Chinook likely *saved my bacon*. This is truly a million-dollar dog!! ** *A story on Chinook appears at 20 September, 1975.*

24 January, 1972

The place still smells of smoke. All my clothes and everything I eat smells or tastes "smoked". I should've hung a few caribou hams in the cabin to cure!

I tore down the chimney and gave it a good scrubbing. That Spruce tree sap is just like roofing tar! Wish I had access to more seasoned dry wood. If I hole up hereabouts next winter I'll surely be better prepared with my wood supply instead of going out and hauling it home every other day.

I am also now keeping blankets and warm clothes at a vacant cabin down the lake. If my cabin should ever catch fire and I have to get out before I can grab my warm clothes, I'll still have this set of "survival" clothes nearby.

Out here one seldom gets a second chance to correct a stupid mistake or an accident. This is a most unforgiving country at times, especially during these brutally cold winters. One must be prepared to face all possible challenges when living alone in a remote area. Or, one must be prepared to perish.

28 January, 1972

Well, I finally have ascertained that I am not the only human left on earth. I have *actually seen* another human!

My regular monthly pilot went "below" on vacation for a few months and the Nears (who have a cabin across the lake) did not make any visits to the lake for a few months due to plane problems, work, weather, etc. Anyhow, before he left in November, Cleo asked me if I wanted him to call someone else to fly in next month and check on me. Well, I said "no", thinking the Nears would likely be flying in once or twice before he returned and would likely bring me in some goodies. Well, that was a *bad* mistake on my part. What's that line about *never* assuming things?

Of course I was OK, but my family and friends certainly didn't know that! Finally my family in Minnesota called the Alaska State Troopers and it was soon all sorted out. Anyhow, almost three months without seeing anyone is a *very long time*! I pretty well ate all of my extra emergency supplies (canned and dried food) as well as hunting and fishing more often.

This was all a lesson learned!

This living alone in the wilderness certainly has a high degree of danger, but this is what I have chosen to do and this is the path I have chosen to walk to achieve this goal of becoming an artist. I graduated college with my art and biology degrees and knew all my life that I wanted to work with wildlife; either through art or with Fish & Game somewhere. I now want this isolation in order to work on my art undisturbed. Art is what I've now decided I want to do for my profession and I know I still have a ways to go. Hopefully I'll have an art show later this spring or summer and sell enough art to provide me with a "grubstake" big enough to let me spend yet another winter somewhere in the bush to continue drawing and painting and studying wildlife. I consider this as *paying my dues* even though this has been a most exciting and fun adventure. I can't imagine any sportsman *not enjoying* what I've seen and done since arriving here in Alaska.

5 June, 1972

Goodbye Mankomen Lake. Thanks for a beautiful and exciting winter. I couldn't resist a look back over my shoulder as the plane flared along the lake shore and watched as the small cabin slowly fade from sight.

On our flight back to Gakona we paused and circled a Black bear that was feeding on a moose calf. Cleo said that most people just don't realize the extent of bear's spring-time killing. The bear (having just recently come out of hibernation) is hungry, food is scarce, and a new-born calf may often make a tempting target. Often a cow will have twins and she isn't able to always protect them both from predators. Wildlife managers often say that *one* is for the specie and *one* is for the predator's specie.

Cow Moose With *Rare* Triplets

15 June, 1972 (*Fairbanks area*)

Spending a lot of time photographing and sketching birds hereabouts. Also, did manage to sell a bunch of my drawings and a few paintings just through a few people I happened to run into. Cool! One person really like my style and called a number of his business friends who also stopped by and did some buying. The biggest painting I sold to a young lady I dated a few times. Was I supposed to charge her less?

Wasn't sure of the proper etiquette on that?

9 July, 1972 (*Kenai/Soldatna*)

Have completely dismembered my sketchbooks of the last few years. I was hoping to keep them forever as a sort of reference file but I discovered that people wanted to buy some of the drawings. Anyhow, I cut them up, had some mats cut, bought some frames and am now selling them. Also, I'm pretty much sold-out of the art I did during my last winter at Mankomen Lake. There may be hope for me yet! ☺

Now, whenever I work in sketchbooks, I'll have to remember to only draw on one side of the page! Just about all of the sketchbook art I framed up also had another drawing on the backside of the page. Wonder how many of my clients will ever find out that there is *another* Lindstrand original on the other side of their framed picture. Such a deal, hey?

2 September, 1972 (*Mankomen Lake*)

Am planning on spending the upcoming winter at Mankomen Lake again; this time at the Farnham's cabin on the lake's east end. This year, also, I'll have some nearby company. Jim and Jo Kruckeberg will be living in their cabin (the one I lived in last winter) and their son Randy and his wife Roxie and their two kids will be living in the neighboring cabin.

Jim has already humbly claimed the title of "mayor". ☺

9 September, 1972

Spent the last two days camped out on a bluff overlooking a wolf den. I think I counted 13 different wolves, ranging from light gray to blackish. Although I stayed a long way away and watched them with binoculars they certainly *knew* I was there.

Only saw a few young wolves. They are certainly a lot bigger than the wolf pups I have previously seen in June. Hunting must be good hereabouts for the pack. Would guess the pups will be following the adult wolves on their hunting trips pretty soon?

13-14 September, 1972

It is cool tonight. Cast from the dock for a half hour or so but no nibbles. Soon the ice will begin to form on the shoreline and then (before freeze-up) the lake trout will bite good. Now, however, the only sure way to get a fish dinner is to walk up the creek and float a fly over a deep hole.

While eating my grayling and hotcake dinner a little earlier, I watched a mink swim across the creek in front of the cabin.

Picked blueberries this morning; plan to freeze up a couple of gallons to use in pancakes and muffins this winter.

A few hunters were hunting out of an old cabin across the way. One of them shot a grizzly that he said "charged him". Of course this is perfectly possible, yet I always have *second thoughts* when these out-of-state hunters are only out for a few days and this happens. I often wonder how many of Alaska's "charging bears" are instead shot from a considerable and safe distance by a hunter who simply wants to "blow a grizzly away" in order to romanticize his hunt and possibly immortalizing himself amongst his cronies back in the beerhalls of Detroit or Tampa or wherever?

Anyhow they stopped by to see if I could help them skin the bear. Since these hunters had no guide or grizzly tag they'll have to surrender the hide and skull to Fish & Game. I didn't even ask them *what* they actually were hunting. Probably a guide just dropped them off to hunt caribou?

Grayling

1 October, 1972

Where else but here, in a little wilderness log cabin, can one so appreciate such simple things as warmth, illumination and food. Things now taken for granted by most of us back in the *civilized* world. Out here one doesn't merely adjust a dial for more heat, or flick on a switch for light, or throw a frozen pizza into the oven for dinner. No, out here one seems to have to *earn* these things. Out here one must fill his lanterns daily (and keep inventory of his supply), must be continually adding to his woodpile to keep his home warm and must live (in part) from the land, a land rich in bounty here. A land which will surely feed him if he is skillful and if he is trained for survival.

11 October, 1972

Have been spending a few hard days hauling firewood out of the hills and down to the lake where it can be "rafted" across to the cabins.

Also, before I forget, the Kruckebergs and I shot a moose down on the lake's western end a while ago. We quartered it and hauled it back to the cabins where it was then hung in the meat sheds and would provide us all with ample winter meat.

The next morning I decided that I wanted the moose head for bait on my winter trap line. Jim and I took his boat down to the kill site and I jumped out of the boat and walked into the brush to retrieve it. Well, it was there and it looked like someone had *sandblasted* the hide and meat off of it! Just the gnawed white skull was left! Also, the gut-pile and hide pieces were gone! Within a time-frame of about 12 hours, grizzlies had found the site and had completely eaten every scrap but the moose's stomach contents.

Well, believe me, my hair stood up on the back of my neck and I boogied out of there *quick*. I would bet you that those grizzlies were still very near! Luckily, Jim was idling the boat and threw it in reverse. That, then, is *HOW* you can get killed by a bear. Stupidly walk into a kill site with no protection! Duh…

16 December, 1972

Early last night (or late afternoon) a pack of wolves came by, snatched an old moose bone from the front yard and moved on. The wolves, three or four, came along the lake edge and zig-zaged around the yard before grabbing the bone and moving on down the creek before they stopped to chew on it.

About ten I had let Chinook out to do his usual before-bed duties. When I went back out later to call him in he was gone. I then noticed all the wolf tracks and saw his tracks following them. I yelled for about ten minutes to no avail. Right then I had a sick feeling in my gut. I just knew that the wolves would be eating tonight.

Anyhow, I bundled up and followed the tracks across the lake and into the brush. After a little more walking and another ten minutes of yelling, I headed home, as surely Chinook would have come to me if he was able. I didn't sleep any and would get out of bed every half hour or so to check if he was at the door.

This morning I got dressed early and called for a while again. I'll have to admit that there was a little *mist* in the ol' eyes about now. To hurry now would be useless, and besides, I wasn't particularly in a rush to bury Chinook's bones and clumps of hair. I ate a *tasteless* breakfast of hotcakes and a moose steak while waiting for a little light to appear. Then I started back on the trail. Soon the trail turned and headed towards a ridge where I knew Jim had set some wolf traps. I turned and headed over to Jim and Jo's cabin and woke them out of bed. I told them the story and drank a cup of coffee while Jim got dressed. Grabbing a .22, we took off towards the ridge and the wolf traps.

There, on the ridge, lay Chinook. His tail was wagging while his left foot was caught in a trap. He actually gave the impression of just waking up from a sound night's snooze! Despite my happiness, I could've beaned him for putting me through this! The trap had caught him high on the paw and when Jim and I released him, he jumped up and ran around like a chicken with its head cut off; none the worse for his last night's adventure.

Now Chinook, his foot clamped in between steel jaws, must've surely yelped? Why didn't the wolves return? Surely the sound of an animal in trouble is music to their ears. Also, why didn't the wolves fall for the bait? Could they smell the traps? Why too did Chinook not fight the trap as a wolf surely would? Was it because the wolf knows nothing but freedom, to roam at will, and to not be restrained for even a moment? Did Chinook accept his captivity much as he might accept the captivity of a collar and chain and so merely laid down and accepted it? All I know is what the tracks tell me. He went for the bait, got his foot caught in the trap, jumped up and down a few times and then lay down in submission. This submission had possibly saved his life, or at least his paw from being mangled.

Looks like I'll have a Merry Christmas after all! ☺ Thank you Lord.

8 March, 1973

"Windows of Wildlife" are these. From these cabin windows I have watched grizzlies, moose, caribou, wolves, fox, mink, wolverine and other odds n' ends of wildlife parading about their wild domain. I have watched cock ptarmigan fighting their aerial spring-time battles across the lake; have watched Peregrine falcons and Bald eagles get baited down to an old moose bone tossed out on the ice. I have laid in bed and watched ravens dive at moose; have watched caribou swim the lake, their hollow hairs making them amongst the best of swimmers. Flocks of swans, geese and sandhill cranes passed over last autumn while I sat inside painting, drawing, or just watching outside.

All this has happened, and all this I have watched through these cabin windows, these "windows of wildlife". No Hollywood movie could even remotely compare with this "*show of shows*".

Trumpeter Swans Migrating

6 September, 1973 (*Moose Creek area*)

Happy days! National Bank of Alaska has commissioned me for a few paintings today. Looks like I'll eat this year again.

Am anxious for the winter to come; I'm itching to paint. My first four paintings are already finished (that is, in my mind!). Now it's merely a matter of going through the fundamentals of putting the scene down on canvas.

Have decided to spend the coming winter up in the Moose Creek area (Petersville area) in a cabin approximately 17 miles west of the Parks highway. It's very rustic but looks snug and has a fantastic view. It is on the south side of a small lake and to the North, towering above the Spruce-studded hills, towers mighty Mount McKinley.

My Winter Cabin

27 April, 1974 (*Beaver Lakes*)

There were a couple of new bird songs in the woods today. Didn't see any of the traveling minstrels but their shrill notes floated through the snow-covered woods and seemed to bring with them a note of urging demands. They too seem to be disgusted with this lingering winter scene. The northcountry is restless, anxious to get on with its job of bearing and raising their various families.

16 June, 1974 (*Pribilof Islands, Bering Sea*)

Flew out to the Pribilof Islands yesterday. St. Paul Island (one of them) is only some 30 square miles in size but is the breeding home to many thousands of fur seals as well as nesting grounds for over 100 different species of birds. Unbelievable place!

Followed an Arctic fox on his rounds today. He was busily killing birds along the steep rookeries. I witnessed him kill one murre and three kittiwakes. The birds are simply *sitting ducks* for a skilled fox. He simply makes a short charge into a batch of nesting birds and kills one, which he then "caches" for pickup later (or perhaps never?) or takes home to his family.

One kittiwake kill was taken home for the young fox kits to play with, tear up and finally eat. They were certainly not famished, as they seemed just as happy for a new plaything as they did for a tasty meal.

The bird rookeries, incidentally, are on sheer cliffs which sometimes rise 200 feet above the sea. A person walking the cliff edge must be ever on the alert for a *weak* shoulder on the ledge. One careless step could easily result in sure death on the rocks below.

20 June, 1974

Spent the day amongst the rookeries, photographing puffins, murres, cormorants, auklets, gulls, kittiwakes and nest-robbing fox. Quite an exciting day on the slopes; nest building, nest robbing, aerial dogfights, family squabbles, etc. etc.

Also watched one fur seal bull drive a bloodied foe out of his territory and into another's territory, where the already injured warrior was again soundly trounced. At one time three neighboring bulls ganged up on him and unmercifully beat him. By the time the bull finally reached the water he was covered in blood. Sharp teeth had slashed and gashed his neck, head and shoulders. I watched him swim out into the fog shrouded sea and disappear.

Found four decomposing seal carcasses at the west end of the Island. All apparent battle casualties? I fear that the one bull I watched get defeated today will also likely become a battle casualty. Out at sea he becomes the helpless prey of killer whales and sharks. If he returns to shore in his weakened condition, he will likely be set upon and killed by the Beachmasters (the breeding bulls) that encircle the island, each with their own jealously-guarded harem of cows.

Today I watched three seal pups being born. The miracle of birth would be unveiled thousands of times here on this small island within the next few weeks. The Island's countless birds and fur seals will soon witness the miracle of life.

The poet, Carl Sandburg, once said that a *baby is God's opinion that the world should go on*.

Horned Puffin

27 August, 1974 *(Anchorage)*

Just read in the paper that a man was killed and eaten by a Brown bear down near Cold Bay. These stories always make me pause in my tracks for a little *reflecting* on my chosen profession.

A person being killed by a bear isn't particularly a novel event in Alaska, but a person being *eaten* by a bear is still, thankfully, quite rare.

29 September, 1974 *(Jack River area)*

Spent the last three days photographing and doing some watercolors of the Alaska Range. In four years I've never seen the mountains as beautiful. A new coat of frost and snow blankets the mountains; their jagged peaks piercing the clear blue sky.

2 October, 1974 *(Anchorage)*

High winds and cold in Anchorage. Wind gusts to 80 mph.

Friday I plan to go out to Big Lake for the weekend. It looks as if Big Lake area will be home for this winter. I have a busy winter planned, including a lot of necessary trips to Anchorage or Fairbanks. Therefore another very remote residence wouldn't work.

My nearest neighbors will be the Lippencotts, about a mile away. I'll be in a cabin on Fish Creek.

4 December, 1974 *(Fish Creek)*

Earlier this evening I was looking through a stack of photographs of drawings and paintings that I had done during the past four years here in Alaska. Well my friend, there *has* been an improvement.

I can't help but look back over my Alaskan years with pride; knowing that I am now beginning to earn a living doing something I want to do: painting and photographing wildlife. This is a good case in point of showing that a person can and will acquire a certain mastery of anything that he has enough interest in and has the willingness and faith to pursue, even if it means living off beans, fish and mooseburgers for a few lean years. A person certainly owes himself the chance.

Although I've seldom any big *lumps* in the bank, I've at least come to eat reasonably regularly as well as being able to drive or hike or fly to most any point in Alaska and staying there for as long as my interest holds me. There always seems to be enough in the *kitty* for that.

5 January, 1975

Was an even -50 early this morning. Records for cold temperatures are being set everyday all around Alaska. Many cities are reporting their lowest temperatures ever recorded for these dates. The cold snap may well last another five days according to the forecasters.

THIS is the time to live out in the "bush. Just throw an extra log in the fire and settle back. Plenty of hot tea, art, or books until the *snap* passes. No electricity outages (as you have none), no having to get cars started, no having to plow through traffic in ice-fog and carbon monoxide. Just *settle back and wait* while the rest of the world keeps things on schedule and the world turning.

Hoarfrost

26 May, 1975 *(Glennallen area)*

20 million shore birds and one million waterfowl are estimated to have moved east through Prince William Sound between April 19 and May 12, 1975. Peak of the goose migration came on May 1st when 11,000 geese passed through.

7 June, 1975 *(Hurricane Gulch area)*

Heading back up to McKinley Nat'l Park to see how the young ones are doing. Most of the ewes should have lambed out by now and the moose cows should've calved. Rainy and cold today.

Met some very boisterous chaps from New Zealand at Mary's McKinley View Lodge. They had just come down after climbing *the* mountain, Denali.

The thing that impressed them the most about America, or at least Alaska, was its abundance of wildlife. In New Zealand they don't have much wildlife, at least nothing in our abundance or variation. They thought we were very lucky to have all these animals.

Yes, we Alaskans are truly lucky, and hopefully we won't ever take our wildlife so "for granted" that we just sit back and think that it'll always be here no matter what we do with our development and environment. After all, these are so called *monstrous days* where technology/development running amuck can almost overnight destroy certain processes of Nature that have taken thousands of years to produce.

9 June, 1975 *(Mt. McKinley Nat'l Park)*

Sure feels good to be up in the hills again. To feel the sweat pour out and to feel the cool breezes and freshness that seems only to exist atop high mountain peaks and ridges. There's a special *exhilaration* that comes from standing on top and looking down over all that spreads out below; the valleys, meadows and twisting rivers.

The lamb crop looks good and most mature ewes have one trailing them. Have spent most of the past two days traveling with and photographing them. Truly, there are few things *cuter* than a newborn lamb!

A few days ago I followed and photographed some Canada geese families around the Anchorage area. A few groups of about 20 goslings each. I think I read somewhere that Canada geese sometimes trade baby-sitting duties with one another? That way the adults can more easily feed, knowing that the "kids" are being looked after. Also, watched two separate pairs of eagles playing in the wind currents above Cook Inlet. How *blessed* I truly am to witness the antics of nature and wildlife almost daily here in *wild* Alaska

Tomorrow it'll have been 5 years since I quit my commercial art job in Minneapolis and began my new life here in Alaska. Wow, what an unbelievable adventure! Certainly no regrets. Also, this year I must decide if I want to continue trying to earn a living as a freelance artist/photographer or get a *real job* in advertising or something.

20 September, 1975 (CHINOOK)

I had often climbed such ridges as the one I now found myself on. Here in Alaska there are thousands of them; some higher or lower than others; some barren or rock strewn; some smothered in wild blueberries and cranberries. Still others were peaceful and wild, covered with thick patches of brush, trees, mountain flowers and fireweed. It was on one such as this that I now stood. The air was branded with the earthy sweetness that follows a heavy summer's rain and the landscape glistened under the now sunny sky. This, then, *was the chosen spot*. This would be where my dog Chinook would be buried. Here, in the wild unsettled country that he learned to call home.

That was in July, during one of my occasional trips into Anchorage. It was getting towards sundown when I pulled off on a little gravel road on the outskirts of town to let Chinook stretch his legs a bit. No sooner had his paws hit the ground than a coyote broke cover in the nearby brush. Before I could react and call him off the chase he had already been swallowed up by the brush.

I set up camp out there and spent the night, quite sure he'd be sleeping under the Bronco when I woke up in the morning. When he wasn't there I began to have some apprehensions, but mostly I simply was angry, as I had just planned on making a quick run into Anchorage to have a camera fixed and then heading back up to Denali where I was photographing a pair of monstrous Dall rams until a bumped cable release ripped the shutter release off the camera body. Knowing how fast sheep can disappear in the mountains made me want to return as soon as possible. And now my dog gets the notion to run down a coyote. Blast!

On the third day I received word from the Alaska S.P.C.A. (Society for the Prevention of Cruelty to Animals) that one of their officers had been contacted by the Anchorage Police Department saying that a dog had been hit and killed by a car. That dog was Chinook. Lacking the experience and wisdom of many "town dogs" for this turf, confused and possibly scared, this "bush dog" found his way onto the highway and was struck down. At 2:45 A.M. on the 31st of July, 1975, Chinook died. I claimed him that next morning at the dog pound and carried him out to that peaceful little hillside to bury him.

The day had turned warm after the earlier rain and by the time I finished smoothing out the dirt on the grave the clouds had given way to some sunshine. I sat down in a patch of fireweed and clover and looked out across the valley; watching the occasional clumps of clouds smash against the mountains. I felt the gentle summer's breeze, heard the distant chattering of a squirrel. And, I cried.

Chinook was truly a *special* dog. A mixed breed with a quarter-wolf ancestry. He was independent, a fighter, a tireless watchdog who occasionally scared people who didn't know him. Perhaps he was more *respected* than *loved*. Perhaps? But, if you'd have asked a child who he'd been pulling around on a sled or had been chasing snowballs for, you'd hear only of love. Tiny hearts know of no *better* word.

Of course all people's dogs are *special* dogs, especially here in the North where dogs are such an important part of our culture. Yet I myself wonder who could possibly have known a dog as well as I did Chinook, or of any two separate species ever bridging the gap of difference as well as we. Every bark and growl of his I seemed to understand. Every whimper. Just by listening to him, I could understand just what animal was skirting or possibly entering camp or approaching one of my various remote cabins. His *moose* bark, for instance, was different than his *bear* bark, which was accompanied by some shivering. Excitement perhaps. Danger. Also, his *treed squirrel* and *approaching person* bark also were in his vocabulary. These barks and growls were like words to me; he was truly my sixth sense, my eyes in the dark. And, as well as I knew him, so I felt he also knew me. We were brothers, a brotherhood obviously not understood by those who have not lived it.

We were friends, good companions. In the winters we'd hole up in some remote cabin. I'd chop the wood and fill the water buckets and he'd haul it home. In the spring we'd board up our various winter quarters and follow and photograph the incoming migrations of waterfowl north. Summers we'd roam the state, exploring it from top to bottom; sometimes by plane, sometimes on foot, sometimes with Bronco or canoe. In the autumn we'd perhaps hunt some and pack it out together. Always it was *us*. Never just *me*. Never just *him*. And now that is no more. Five good years we had spent together here in Alaska. Today would be our last moments together. *I would not return to disturb him*.

Yes, five years of constant companionship. Five years of memories; some good, some happy, some sad, some downright scarey. There were times when we were lost in the wilds and lived for days on fish and berries. There was the time we flew into a remote lake for a week and ended up on opposite sides of an enraged grizzly who wandered down into camp. There was the time we rode a punctured, spinning raft downstream until finally grounding ourselves on a bar. There was the time that wolves came into our yard out at Mankomen Lake and he followed their tracks and ended up in a wolf trap a few miles away. Then there was the time he was trampled by a cow moose in the deep snow a few feet from another winter cabin. Yes, some of our times together were downright scary! Also, truthfully, I'd guess I wouldn't even be around today if it wasn't for my buddy.

There were less exciting times too of course; times which one remembers now best of all. Times of just loafing around or enjoying a snooze in the warm sun. Times when I'd be sitting in a snug winter cabin working on some art and he'd rise from his rug bed, stretch, and come over and lay his snoot on my knee and whine for a little pat. Or, of the times I'd hook him up to his harness, attach a tow rope, climb on my skis and mush him down some trail. I remember too how he liked to roughhouse with kids or haul them around on sleds. Or of the days he literally baby-sat an injured Hawk owl until it recovered enough to fly away. And then there was the matter of those *big brown eyes* of his.

So, this then was Chinook, a dog of the north. A dog who lived only a handful of years but who made an impression upon those he touched by his mere presence.

So, my friend, I sadly bid you goodbye. Soon the brush and flowers will grow up over your grave and the spot will be forgotten, as wild and unmarked as it was meant to be. With time I will perhaps think of you less, for such is the way of time. Yet, whenever I hear a wolf howl tumble across the tundra or watch a band of caribou run free, or lay back some night and look up at the stars and Northern Lights, I'll likely think of you. And, although a tear may run down my cheek, I'll smile and thank you for being just what you were. A friend.

Goodbye my friend.

Chinook

2 November, 1975 (*Goose Creek*)

Have set up winter quarters at a cabin on Goose Creek, a few miles west of the Talkeetna cut-off.

Still clear and cold. Been so for about a week now. Spent the past few days bucking up the woodpile. A few more days of it and I'll be able to hang up the ol' axe for awhile.

I have somewhat covered the length and width of this world of ours; from Tahiti to Minnesota and from Mexico to Singapore. Yet, it was not until two days ago that I discovered one of the world's most *enlightening* secrets. That *enlightenment* being a Styrofoam outhouse seat. INSTANT warmth! Try it, you'll like it!

Somehow the coming winter doesn't seem nearly as harsh as my previous five Alaska winters. ☺

2 October, 1976 (*West Beaver Lake*)

Have bought a home. Perhaps it is an attempt on my part to begin to put down some roots?

I have spent each of the past six winters at different cabins around Alaska, feeling that the change of environment and scenery was a necessity needed to help me learn about Alaska's varied wildlife and to also help me grow as an artist. However, now with my decision to put out my first book, I have found it somewhat necessary to be in a place where I could stay in touch with my publisher. I have now entered the *scary world* of telephones, home payments and possible electricity outages.

Here on the shores of a small lake in the Mat-Su Valley, I will try this *new* lifestyle. My backpack is still packed if this lifestyle doesn't work out.....

27 April, 1978 (*Goose Bay*)

I'm impressed! Saw hundreds of swans bunched up throughout Goose Bay (near Knik, AK.). Also, lots of ducks and geese. Would imagine this area to be a resting and gathering spot for the waterfowl before they mostly head north to their own particular nesting sites. Hope to spend the next few days crawling around out here with my camera.

Saw a Sparrow hawk out south of Palmer with a small bird in its talons. Also, at Goose Bay, I watched as every duck, goose and swan seemed to rise when a single Bald eagle flew over. Boy, what terror those birds of prey must bring!

Bald Eagle

22-25 November, 1978 (*enroute to Haines*)

Left home heading North. Weather turned absolutely lousy towards Willow and I fought a blizzard and icy roads all the way up to Fairbanks. Wanted to get some winter shots of the Alaska Range and also of Mt. McKinley (also called "Denali" by many). Didn't get the blue sky I was hoping for however.

The next day I headed to Tok and then started down to Haines to photograph and sketch the gathering of Bald eagles that occurs there this time of year. Thousands of eagles bunch up in that area to fish for the salmon that are still running in the unfrozen creeks.

Haines. Lots of baldies around. Must have seen nearly 1,000 eagles today. Went hiking along the rivers most of the day. A slight drizzle fell on and off and the shootin' light was poor.

A lot of buffleheads and goldeneyes in the bays hereabouts; all swimming around in huge "rafts".

Would like to get back here during the hooligan (a small smelt-like fish) run in the spring (about May 13th or so according to Bea S. of Haines) as then the sealions and otters and whales seem to congregate en'mass for some good meals.

Peaceful night. Sitting here across the bay from Haines tonight watching the little town's lights sparkle and dance on the rippling ocean. Nice town, nice people.

Winter landscape near Sheep Mt. / Eureka

6 February, 1979 (*West Beaver Lake*)

Spent the better part of the morning following a Saw-whet owl around the woods. Firstly spotted him as I walked out on the lake ice for my morning's look up and down the lake. He was so intent on hunting shrews at my woodpile that I walked within an arm's length of him. Only when I said "*Good morning Big Eyes*" did he pivot his head and give me a few seconds of attention.

Hope he got his morning's "ham and eggs" (shrews).

A thought. Wilderness air: so fresh and clean, as though it's never been *used* before.

12 February, 1979

State game biologists are planning to move about 40 upper Nelchina Basin Brown bears this coming spring. The idea is to have them removed during the two or three weeks of moose calving in the area.

The belief is that bears are causing the 70 % death rate of newborn moose. This experiment of moving the bears should either confirm or disprove this belief. An earlier project of thinning out the wolves in the area didn't seem to help prevent the high death rate amongst the area's moose calves. Therefore, the Brown bear/grizzly became the prime suspect.

During the two year study, biologists attached radios to 122 newborn moose. Sixty-five of those calves died. Of these at least 52 were killed by bears. The rest died by either bears, wolves or various accidents.

Although the bears have a strong *homing* instinct and most will eventually return to their former range, they are being moved far enough away that when they do return it will be after the *critical* period for moose calves.

28 October, 1979

6" of snow fell last night. Winter wonderland! Trees are drooping with thick white blankets. Lake has a slushy ice covering about half-way out. A huge flock of about 200 goldeneyes on the lake.

A great day here in the north country. Went walking on snowshoes. Someone once said that there are some who can live without wild things and some who cannot. I certainly cannot.

To be the sole owner of all that passes beneath one's feet, unbounded and unshackled in spirit, that is the beauty of walking Alaska's wilds.

Winter Wonderland

A Red Fox Curls Up In The Snow

20 December, 1979

Have now *officially* gotten back into dog mushing. Have acquired four dogs. All of them are old enough to qualify for Social Security I think…

"Buck" is a good ol' boy. 60 lbs, friendly and about as smart as a bag of rocks. "Shakey" is white, 60 lbs and kind've *shakey*. Hard to get too friendly with yet as he is pretty nervous. May have had a tough life with a previous musher? "Silver" is about 40 pounds and will likely give you a nip if you turn your back on him. "Spooky" is a leader. 50 lbs of determined *boss*! Think he'll be a good one.

28 December, 1979

Have added two young dogs to the team. Grifter and Crystal. 1-1/2 year old brother and sister. Do they ever love to run! When I hook them up to the sled they just bounce up and down howling until I yell "Mush" and we're off like a bullet.

Beautiful day to run dogs and enjoy the great winter outdoors. Nothing to break the peaceful silence but the *whoosh* of the sled runners over the snow.

Ran the team on a 20 mile trail the other night under a sky smothered with stars. Takes a while to adjust to the night's light but pretty soon you can see most everything along the familiar trail.

26 April, 1980 (Kenai area)

Snow geese peaked around April 22nd here on the Kenai flats. Most have already departed for their nesting grounds in Siberia.

7 August, 1980 (Montana Creek)

Dad said today that this was the first time he can remember ever getting tired of catching fish! Yet he kept fishing. Tired yes, but not *too tired* to QUIT! ☺

What a great run of pink, chum and silver salmon this year in the Upper Cook Inlet drainage.

Silver Salmon

12 September, 1980 (Fairbanks)

Autumn comes to us with a sort of subtlety and yet with a sense of shock. It is upon our first notice of a golden aspen leaf in the sea of green forest that we realize summer has bid us adieu.

27 September, 1980 (West Beaver Lake)

Spent a few hours cleaning ducks with Jeff Bussler of Minnesota. We just returned after spending a few days hunting ducks out on the Susitna Flats.

Have to get started cutting and stacking wood. The water level here at the lake is about 6" higher than the past few years because of all our rain. The beavers have dammed the creek at the lake's south end and the top of my dock is only about 2" above the water level.

Al Capp (the famous cartoonist) once summed up my feelings on abstract art: "A product of the untalented, sold by the unprincipled to the utterly bewildered." That's funny. ☺

Wonder which of my artist-friends I'll lose after writing this?

17 December, 1980

Both water pipes under the cabin broke. It has been about 40 below these past few days and yesterday I noticed that the pipes were frozen. I heated the crawl-space with a heater and when the pipes thawed they burst. It is during times such as this that I yearn for the *simpler times* of my Alaskan life. Times when I didn't worry about "frozen pipes" (and similar luxuries) and just went out to the lake and dipped out a bucket of water from my ice hole.

40 below weather is supposed to hold for a while longer. The daytime sky is a light blue and pink. The mountains have a crisp, clean look. Also, only about 5" of snow on the ground. We dog-mushers desperately need another foot or two of that white stuff.

21 February, 1981

About 4" of snow last night. Ran the dogs on my usual 20 mile loop. Am now running only 5 dogs as 3 of my dogs aren't working out at present. Buffy won't run on any slippery surface and will tangle up the whole team by dragging herself, and Bandit and Kelly just won't keep a tight harness and instead just let the other dogs do all the work. Wonder *why* I got these dogs *free* from my mushing friends? Oh well, I've got time and patience….

Am still running Spooky in lead. He is not as fast as Maruska but is a better Gee/Haw leader (that is, he is better at taking verbal commands) than she is.

I'm running Maruska and Sugar in swing. Both excellent dogs. Sugar will chew on the ropes if you hook her up and keep her waiting too long before you start mushing. I have to hook her up last and then be ready to "hit the trail" instantly. Maruska just stands there and howls, she wants to run so bad. Buck and Brownie are my good wheel-dogs (right in front of the sled).

9 dogs is the max I want to run in one team. Too tough to keep a bigger team from getting tangled up or from fighting amongst themselves. This mushing is, after all, just entertainment for me.

28 April, 1981

Just got the OK from the Public Communications section of the Alaska Department of Fish & Game to reproduce their "Wildlife Notebook Series" in the new edition of my Alaska Sketchbook. My original plan was to write up all the animal information myself, but if I had it wouldn't have been as *factual and accurate* as if written by these ADF & G biologists and professionals who deal specifically with these various individual animals.

I thank them for helping make this Alaska Sketchbook a *better thing*.

28 May, 1981 (Portage Glacier area)

While heading out to the Portage Glacier area I stopped at Potter Marsh. Watched a pair of Horned grebes perform a bit of their mating rituals. The two would belly up to each other in the water and then stretch out their necks and point their beaks skyward, all the while "cooing" their grebe call.

Out glassing and photographing birds while hiking the area. Threw a Snickers and apple in the backpack and hit the trail. Have also been taking pictures of the glaciers here. Sure are *blue*!

The glacier ice is blue, incidentally, because it has had the air squeezed out of it by the weight of years and years of snow. The crystals that are formed from this compression absorb most of the colors of the spectrum but reflect *blue*. Or something like that…I think…

Portage Glacier

12-14 June, 1981 (*Susitna & Deshka Rivers*)

My cousin Gene and his son Kyle have spent a few days fishing here on the Deshka with me. So far have only caught 5 Kings, the biggest being about 35#'s.

We woke up this morning in water! The river rose some 6-8" overnight and flooded our campsite. Gene said he rolled over in his sleeping bag, heard a *squish-squish* sound and decided it was time to get up. Next time we'll camp on higher ground as we normally do. But then, who'd expect the river to rise that much overnight?

Miserable boat ride down the Big Su to the Deshka. Cold rain stung our faces as we headed to our fishing hole in my open Zodiak (no windshield or roof). We did pause a few minutes at a dead, bloated moose that had a few ravens and eagles feeding on it.

20 June, 1981 (*West Beaver Lake*)

To become a wildlife artist, there is no place to go but to Nature itself. Only then can one find the answers to what it is he seeks. No books or lectures can teach a young artist like the teachings to be found at Nature's hand and in her wild realm.

We must never forget one of Nature's basic lessons: that life depends upon life and that everything is part of something greater. Walking along the shores of the Little Susitna River the other day reminded me of it so effectively. It is what we now call an ecosystem, the sum of all the related parts. If not disturbed by man's *management*, it will likely run forever. Rivers, sun, willows, moose and wolves are all connected in this ecosystem.

29 August, 1981 (*Susitna River*)

I swear there should be an *open season* on airboats! Every fisherman and hunter should be allowed to sink all they want!

Seriously, the things are a real irritant; they're an intrusion on every sportsman and other human being within miles of them.

They roar by with such a noise that every moose and wild creature in the area simply flees. Can you imagine having *putted* a little boat ten miles down some wild river to enjoy some peaceful fishing and photography only to almost be run down at your journey's end by a pair of inconsiderate and completely careless airboaters! And, after almost swamping me, not even pausing to look back to make sure I'm OK?...An *elementary* courtesy one human being should certainly extend to another! It was as if they had the right-of-way on the river simply because they were *bigger* and *faster*!

I'm sure I speak for many, many sportsmen and outdoor folks when I speak of my low regard for the "bullies" of the rivers (as well as the rest of the great outdoors) who seemingly have absolutely no regard for others. I have watched airboats (as well as other jet boats) come flying down rivers and around blind-curves at full speed and with no regard for people fishing from shore in hip-boots. Hats fly, hipboots fill and tempers flare! Someday two of these boats (coming from opposite directions) are certainly going to collide on one of those blind curves and kill everyone.

1 February, 1982 (*West Beaver Lakes*)

Running into some heavy snow on some of my trails and have to walk ahead of the dogs to break trail for them. Spooky is a good leader and will usually keep the team a few steps in back of me and so isn't constantly stepping on the backs of my snowshoes the way Maruska does. She's one of those dogs that just can't seem to get *close enough*, you know? I swear she should've been a cat instead of a dog! She's a dog that seems to *purr* instead of bark. ☺

Camped overnight last night in a stand of Spruce near the Little Susitna River. Running a small team of seven dogs. Got the team chained and fed, set up the tent, and put the tea water on. Cold but not miserable if you're dressed for winter camping.

Fox and rabbit tracks are fairly scarce hereabouts, *but* moose tracks *and* moose are everywhere it seems. I've had a couple of exciting rides through the woods when we ran up on a moose on our trail. About all one can do is ride the brake, yell "WHOA you no-good-so-and-so's" (or something) and hang on for dear life!

Had time to sit by the campfire and watch the stars before bedding down. What a peaceful site. Can't help but think about what *freedom* I enjoy here in Alaska and sometimes take for granted. However, I think I appreciate this *freedom* as much as anyone can. The freedom to choose our own *path* in life. Perhaps I appreciate it so deeply is partly because I have spent time in the jungles of Vietnam where men and women died to protect these rights and also having traveled to other parts of the world where such "freedoms" are denied its citizens.

Freedom, after all, is *not free*. Once you've seen the *other side of the mountain* you may yearn to return home and never leave.

Author with (L-R) Silver, Shakey, Spooky and Buck.

21 July, 1982 (*Kenai*)

A great day on the river today! My friend Patti, Dad, Lori Collins (my neice) and I each caught a King. A 62#'er for Patti (her 1st King salmon) and a 50#, 45#, and 22#'er for the rest of us. You can probably guess who caught the *little one*? ☹ I take my little lady friend out to show her *how to do it* and the biggest battle I have all day is holding her in the boat while she reels in her "snag"!

Anyhow, Dad and Lori have a fish cooler full for their trip back to Minnesota.

31 August, 1982 (*Beaver Lakes*)

Poured rain these last few days. A bumper crop of mushrooms growing here in this damp weather and the little red squirrels are stashing them all over in the trees. You can look up in some trees and it looks like a mushroom farm! Busy as beavers they are.

Lowbush cranberries are almost ready to pick. Starting to turn dark maroon. They are as thick as rocks on a country road. Plenty of blueberries too. Frost can't be too far away anymore.

15 November, 1982 (*Hawaii*)

Patti and I got married. Will live happily ever after I'm sure. A beautiful ceremony in Hawaii; outside in a little chapel amidst waterfalls, lush flowers, tropical birds and plenty of sunshine.

Southern girl and Yankee boy. Opposites attract?

14 March, 1983 (*Anchorage*)

A sad day for me today. Just received word that my friend "Citico Charlie" Hodges has passed away. He was the sourdough model for many of my paintings and is, in fact, on the cover of my first "Alaskan Sketchbook".

His wish was to be cremated and his ashes scattered on the glaciers of Mt. McKinley. He said: "*The view from there will be just fine.*"

25 April, 1983 (Kenai Peninsula)

Snow geese everywhere lately. Huge flocks. Also, swans on the Moose River which I floated a canoe through and photographed without spooking. A lot of ducks and terns and one Snowy owl hunting the salt flats outside Kenai. It probably is on the prowl for sick or injured ducks and geese.

The ducks and birds aren't nearly as afraid of me as they are of that owl flying around. If he passes anywhere near a flock, off they go. The owl is the *prophet of doom* to them. Beware the grim reaper!

Great to see the land once again awaken from the long sleep of winter.

Snow Geese

3 December, 1983 (West Beaver Lake)

Hazel Heath of Homer gave me a call yesterday telling me that President Reagan was given one of my Alaska Sketchbooks on his stop in Anchorage. She called to *make my day*, which she certainly did!

To think that your own little book was considered worthy enough to be given to the President of the United States as one of the representatives of this great state of Alaska is indeed an honor.

I think I'll sit down and smile for awhile…

20 December, 1983

Chopped down a little Christmas tree this morning. Snow still covering the Spruce trees in the woods. No winds lately to blow the beautiful "winter wonderland look" away. About 0 degrees today.

Things have been so busy lately for Patti and I (business) that it's just been the last few days that we've been able to relax and enjoy this Christmas season. So, today I headed out into the woods with my trusty ax and Patti started getting the wreaths and tree decorations out. Tomorrow we *deck the halls with balls of holly*….

11 January, 1984

Just finished reading an article put out by Fish & Game called "Wolf - Prey Relationships in Interior Alaska".

Its conclusion: predation by wolves was a major factor in the crashes and continued low population levels in many of Alaska's big game herds. The Department, beginning with Statehood, phased out wolf control, protected wolves and considered them a desired component of Alaska's native fauna and emphasized that wolves were not a major limiting factor on Alaska's big game herds. In the mid-70's, however, the Department reversed their thinking and began wolf control programs to try and help the game recover their numbers.

Interesting article and worth reading for all who are interested in our wildlife; the concept of *balance of nature* as opposed to *control by the intervention of man*.

**** Unfortunately, have somehow and somewhere lost years of journal entries. ☹ Am now picking up in 1994.

3 June, 1995 (Hwy 4 to Valdez)

A Black bear crossed the highway (near Milepost 50) carrying a large swan in its mouth. The swan was so big that the bear was dragging it as he walked into the brush. No photos (of course!) as he crossed before I could get pulled over and shoot. Truly one of my most spectacular wildlife sightings in Alaska. My guess is that the swan (Trumpeter?) was likely protecting a nest and thus became vulnerable?

29 March, 2000 (Anchorage)

The Big Snow!! Anchorage had about 3 feet of snow dumped on it in 24 hours. Almost TWICE the previous record one-day snowfall. Get the shovel out…. However, downhill and cross-country skiers are certainly rejoicing.

12 April, 2000 (Southcentral Alaska)

A few dozen seagulls south of Anchorage and big flocks of Canada geese have arrived hereabouts. Most of the ponds and lakes are still frozen and the ground is still snow-covered. C'mon Spring! Break!

19 August, 2000 (quick run South)

Decided to head south for a few weeks to work on a few new books on North American wildlife. Need additional reference material on such species as Bighorns, Mountain lions, Elk, Whitetails and Pronghorns. I sort've hate to leave Alaska at this spectacular time of year but want to get into Canada while the elk are in the rut and also film and sketch the different species of sheep down through Canada and further south.

Spent a few weeks traveling about; Jasper & Banff National Parks in Alberta and then south to Yellowstone and the Grand Tetons. Definitely picked up a lot of reference material; wildlife & landscape.

Whitetail Buck

5 June, 2001

Wow, it's now been about 30 years of running around hereabouts and doing my art/photography. I've been one of the truly lucky ones who's been fortunate to do what he wanted to do with his life and was able to earn a living while doing it. Over the years I have traveled up and down and across Alaska and North America. It has been an honor to walk free across the lands, breath in the fresh air of the wilderness and gaze upon the magnificence of its many treasures. *What an adventure*!!

25/27 September, 2001 (quick run into Canada)

Left Anchorage at noon after spending a few hours following a young bull moose and two cows around the Potter Marsh area. The bull was clearly interested in the adult cows but they would only run away whenever he approached.

Splashes of sunshine on and off today after the past few days of rain and wind. The white Dall sheep that browsed along the rocky mountains of Turnagain Arm stood out against the brilliant autumn colors of that area.

The ponds of Glennallen and Tok have their edges ringed in ice from the recent nighttime freezes and small groups of Trumpeter swans were stopping to feed in them as they migrated South for the winter.

Small bands of caribou crossed the marshy tundra in the Eureka area; perhaps following the same trails as countless generations before them. Trees near Tok are bare of leaves, while those near Anchorage still had most of their colorful leaves.

Termination dust (snow) has covered the mountain tops east of Anchorage the past few days.

A brilliant red dawn on the 26th. A lone wolf paused to look back at my approaching vehicle before turning off the highway shoulder and disappearing into the brush.

Mostly blue sky as I drive east on the 27th. Kluane Nat'l Park, Yukon still had colorful hills despite the snow that had descended halfway down the mountain slopes. When I glassed the Dall sheep near Sheep Mountain in the Yukon, I saw 4 ravens dive-bombing a small band of sheep until the sheep left. Either the ravens were playing a game at the sheep's expense or they wanted the high rocky hill as their own observation point.

29 December, 2001 (Anchorage)

Read that more than 50 caribou of the Killey River herd were killed in an avalanche in the Kenai mountains earlier this month. A very unusual act of nature as far as caribou are concerned; this more commonly happens to sheep and Mountain goats. Biologists concluded that the band of caribou were traversing a steep, snowy and treeless ridge and triggered the slide.

25 April, 2002 (Mat-Su Valley)

Geese are migrating into the Matanuska / Susitna valleys the past few days. Snow geese and Canada geese. Most Snow geese I've ever seen in the Palmer area. There were only a few Snows on the Kenai flats yesterday but then they haven't bunched up there for the last 10 years or so. In the "olden days" the tideflats were just "white" with thousands of Snow geese.

Male Willow Ptarmigan

18 May, 2002 (Denali Nat'l Park)

High 60's. Perfect sunny days for camping and hiking. The Willow ptarmigan are establishing their nesting territories, the pussy willows are blooming and the creeks are breaking up. No better place to be than in the Alaska wilderness on days like this. Think I'll stick around awhile.

22 May, 2002 (Anchorage)

Have had about 10 days of "perfect" weather lately. 60-70 and sunny. Watched two raven's nests perched high in the rocks of the ocean edge. Will move in closer in a week or so after the chicks are larger. The nests are built so no land access is possible but hope to shoot across the ravine with my large 600mm lens.

Saw my first moose calf of the year on the lower hillside.

24 May, 2002 (Central Alaska)

Camped on the east shore of Paxson lake. TOO hot; 80's. A slight breeze so the bugs aren't bad. A few fishermen are fishing the lake's edge for lake trout. The lake is still ice-covered except for about 50 feet out from the shoreline. There were about 4 or 5 other campers around.

Hoping Alaska has a good tourist season this summer. After 9/11 a lot of people cancelled tours, flights, RV rentals, etc. However, Alaska has surely got to be one of the safest places in the world to vacation, hey?

America has always been "vulnerable" to this type of cowardly act because of our free and open society. We must now be ever vigilant but also strive to vigorously protect the ideals that made us the world's freest and greatest Nation. Hopefully most Americans will never forget that freedom is not free but must be earned. And, those who have given their "all" so that we can be free must NEVER be forgotten!

Towards nightfall a young bull moose passed my campsite at the water's edge. He passed so close that the glow of the campfire cast a yellow-red hue on his coat. Gave me a *bit of a start* as I firstly thought it was a grizzly come calling!

Couldn't help but think of a photographer friend, Michio Hoshino, who was killed by a bear while shootin' in Russia in 1996 (date?). Evidently, a young bear attacked him while he was sleeping in his tent. He was only about 40? Only photographed with him twice up in Denali National Park. *Very* passionate about his wildlife photography! Fun guy to hike and photograph with. Died doing what he loved doing.

29 May, 2002 (Windy Point, s. of Anchorage)

This is one of those times when a "starving" wildlife artist/photographer is thrilled to live in Alaska and live the life he lives. I'm presently sitting atop a ridge near Windy Point and less than a mile from the Seward highway. In the rocks across a ravine a pair of adult ravens are diving in and out of their nest while feeding a squawking and demanding chick. Three Dall rams are browsing on the young tree buds and bushes of the lower slopes. Two are full-curl rams and one is 3/4 curl. Fifty yards above them are 4 ewes with 2 newly born lambs bedded on a grassy knoll. These lambs are probably only a few days (or hours?) old. Further south I glassed another half-dozen ewes and yearlings. Above me Bald eagles soar over the ocean's shoreline and occasionally land on exposed sandbars. Wild flowers are coloring the gentle slopes with yellows and blues. Also, blue sky and 70's (and NO bugs!)

Yes, this is a great day to be self-employed!

30 May, 2002 (20 Mile river)

Hooligan dippers are scooping up the little fish by the buckets. The fish are migrating up the river right now and some "tides" are full of fish. Drizzle and cold today. Off to Homer to photograph Eider ducks that often nest in the driftwood snags on the beach. Still a lot of snow up in Turnagain Pass. Watched one newborn moose calf struggle thru a stretch of snow while following its Mom up a trail. It kept bellying-out in the snow because of its short legs. Poor little guy.

31 May, 2002 (Kenai Peninsula)

Buds are opening up and the hillsides are greening up, seemingly overnight! Another week or so and summer should be in full bloom. Lupine flowers are coloring the roadsides.

222 moose were killed on the roads of the Kenai this past winter.

President Bush announced on the radio that $235,000,000 would be spent to buy out mineral rights in the cypress swamps of the Everglades and off the white-sand beaches of the Gulf of Mexico, thus protecting these natural treasures. This will help protect some of the last refuges of the endangered Florida panther.

3 June, 2002 (Anchorage area)

Photographed the first goslings and ducklings sighted this year. There are a few Bald eagles and at least one Red fox patrolling the Potter Marsh area looking for young and easy prey. *They'd best not stray from their protective parents!*

"Banded" Canada Goose and Goslings

6 June, 2002 (Windy Point)

5 rams and 2 ewes were roaming and feeding in the Windy Point area (about mile 107 Seward Hwy.). Was able to get very close by moving slowly and sitting down when they seemed fidgety. 2 of the rams were full-curl or better. Good photos.

9- 10 June, 2002 (Denali Nat'l Park)

Off to Denali. Was lucky enough to get a photographer's pass in the "lottery". Partly cloudy but Mount McKinley is "out". 1st good view is about Mile 11 on the park road. 2nd good view is about at Mile 16. The sun turned to rain in the afternoon. Also, I don't think I've ever seen as many mosquitoes as today!! With the blood I'm donating to them I may well be "history" by dawn….

Two 2 1/2 year old grizzly cubs and their Mom browsed and grazed around my vehicle for about an hour. VERY exciting to watch from so close. GOOD photos too. A few buses pulled alongside and the tourists leaning out the windows were shooting film and popping flashbulbs like it was the 4th of July. I'll bet this "made their day" like it did mine. Momma bear kept an eye on her kids as they circled our vehicles but mainly just occupied herself with feeding. I did start up my car and backed up when one cub began to chew on my bumper. They were both beautifully colored "Toklat blonde" bears.

A bunch of Snowshoe hares in Sanctuary campground. Spruce grouse in Riley Creek campground. Rock ptarmigan in Toklat Pass area. The males, unlike the area's Willow ptarmigan, still seem to be establishing their mating territories. Whenever one cock ptarmigan hears another ones "cackle" he'll fly over that way to chase off the intruder.

A very large bodied bull moose at mile 33. Very large antlers for this early in June. He'll likely be a real monster by September. Was very aggressive too (or inquisitive?) as he constantly kept coming towards me as I moved about for photographs. Usually their sensitive-velvet-covered antlers will dissuade them from challenging anything unless really threatened (as with wolves) and then they normally use their front feet as weapons.

Windy later in the day. Helped keep the mosquitoes grounded. Six large rams were high above Polychrome Pass. Will hike up there tomorrow if they move out of sight. I don't like to move animals if they are in view of the road as the busloads of people want to seem them too and often don't have the opportunity (like I do) of hiking up to them.

The next morning (10th) I hiked up there and found them on a distant hill. Too much "bad" country between us and so I returned downhill.

Raining hard! Guess I'll catch up on notes and finish a few sketches I started in the high country earlier. A few bands of caribou are passing through the area.

Rained "off and on" on the 11th and 12th too. Spent the days stoking campfires and also sketching bears in my tent. Meals: marshmallows, hot chocolate and fire- blackened hotdogs. Yum!

Cow Moose and Calves

13 - 16 June, 2002 (Denali to Anchorage)

Made a quick run to Anchorage and back again. Wanted to process some film to see what it looked like and to give me an idea of what I should shoot (or reshoot) next. All looked OK. I did "push" most of my Provia 100 to 200 ASA because of the poor light. I am shooting one camera at + 1/3 stop and bracketing it by .5. My other camera shoots OK as is and I bracket my shots with it too.

Ran into Leo & Dorothy Keeler along the park road. They were there photographing wolves. We also ran into Gordon Haber later in Sable Pass. Gordon is probably the person that has the most knowledge of the wolves of Denali as he has been studying them for a number of years now. Told us a story of a porcupine crawling down a den hole that had wolf pups inside and at least one of the adults got severely "quilled up" while trying to expel it. That could be *big trouble* for these young pups and possibly for the wolf pack overall. Nature can seem very cruel at times, hey?

Glassed a sow with spring cubs later in the afternoon. They were staying up high in the hills as the boars were mostly down low and feeding along the creeks and valleys. Mother bears usually stay up high with their new cubs so as not to bump into them until the cubs are older and faster. Male bears will often kill cubs if they can catch them; a situation that I have witnessed twice already while traveling in bear country.

Next day: Watched two mating grizzlies at Stony Point. During their actual mating the boar raked the face of the female as she struggled to uncouple. The boar than took off running. Must've run a mile at full sprint before he disappeared over a ridge and out of sight. *Very strange behavior!* The sow was bleeding from her nose and cheek area but evidently both eyes were OK. Later, further down the road I glassed a male pursuing a smaller bear (likely a female) but she kept ahead of it. Every so often he would stop and lay down and then she too would stop to eat until he again pursued her.

Next day: Watched a few bands of Dall sheep crossing from one mountain to another in the Toklat area. The sheep are very vulnerable when they are down low and so make these crossings very fast. If wolves were to catch them here they would likely be able to kill some before they could escape to the safety of the rocky high country.

A few photos of a single wolf near Polychrome Pass.

Sheep Crosssing *Dangerous* Low Country

7 September, 2002 (Denali)

Autumn colors are in full brilliance! Trees and brush are a mixture of yellows, greens, oranges and reds. Spectacular. I'll likely hang around the area for a week or so and do some drawing and photography. The long range forecast is for rain but today, however, we had moments of blue sky mixed in with passing showers.

The moose are beginning to bunch up in small herds. Saw one herd of 6 cows and one herd of 7 cows. There were a few bulls on the fringes but they didn't seem to have any interest in the cows yet. A few bulls were practice fighting so guess the annual "rut" isn't really in full charge yet. Soon the larger bulls will seek out a herd of cows to mate with and will then drive away younger or weaker opponents with serious battles. Usually the defeated bull isn't seriously injured and retreats when his defeat is evident. I have, however, seen two large bulls "ambushed" by a third bull while fighting with another one. The third bull (on both occasions) would charge into one of the fighting bulls and spear it in its side, thus likely breaking ribs, etc. A "cheap shot" but quickly putting the unlucky bull out of contention and possibly causing its early death.

Ptarmigan are in their autumn camouflaged colors.

9th. A little snow has fallen in the high country the past few days. Caribou have their magnificent autumn coats on now too. White necks and polished antlers. Been in the 30's to 50's and most of the leaves have now fallen off the brush and trees. Makes spotting wildlife easier but the terrain colors are really what completes a great animal photograph. Guess I'll hit the road and head back to town and my studio soon.

4 May, 2003 *(south of Girdwood)*

Spotted a Sitka Black-tailed deer walking along the railroad tracks south of Girdwood. Although there have been rumors that a few deer were moving into our area no one had ever taken a photograph of one. My photo did make the front page of the Anchorage Daily News and was also sold to the Associated Press.

The reason we don't have deer here near Anchorage is because their short legs wouldn't get them through our normally deep snows. Moose, however, have long legs and thrive hereabouts.

19 May, 2003 *(Turnagain Arm)*

A Gray whale died and washed up on shore in Turnagain Arm. Every year or so a large whale dies naturally or dies after getting stranded at low tide in the Arm. Once their massive weight isn't supported by water they evidently get their insides crushed. Beluga whales, however, are smaller and lighter and if rescuers can reach them after they have become stranded by a low tide, they can usually be saved until the rising tide carries them away. Whales sunburn easily and must be covered with blankets that are continuously soaked in seawater.

5/6 June, 2003 *(Eagleglen Golf Course, Elmendorf AFB)*

Spent the past two days photographing Red fox near their den on a golf course in the Anchorage area. The fox family had a den underneath a boardwalk that crossed a wet area in front of the Par 3, 17th hole. There were 7 kits there at one time but lately the golfers and course marshals have only noticed 5. Eagles and coyotes have been known to grab the careless ones before they can reach the safely of their holes.

Whenever a golfer would hit his tee shot at the green and the ball would strike leaves or trees before falling, one or two young fox would run out and snatch the ball and run away with it. Rumor has it that over 100 golf balls were fished out of one den hole later in the year.

Anyhow, got some great shots of the fox running with golf balls in their mouths. Needed patience though as the kits would often disappear for hours to nap in their den.

Fox Kit With Golf Ball

8 June, 2003 *(Hillside, Anchorage area)*

Two moose calves have been killed by Brown bears on the Hillside these past few days. An effective bear can be devastating to an area's spring moose calf survival. Once a bear learns the technique of separating a calf from its protective mother he can do it the rest of his life. Bears are ravenous at this time of year and can probably eat a newborn calf in one day.

14 June, 2003 *(Potter Marsh)*

I think that a nest of Horned grebe chicks hatched yesterday. The chicks were still sitting in the nest but the incubating adult was gone. Later I saw both adults down the pond diving for insects and minnows. Also, make note; saw 1st Canada geese goslings on June 1st and saw 1st Mallard chicks and Mew gull chicks on June 7th.

18 June, 2003 *(Mile 101 Parks Hwy.)*

Trumpeter swan nest near Parks highway. Three chicks are swimming around with the adults. I photographed one nest near Glennallen over a 4th of July weekend one year and I think the chick there was smaller than these chicks. Guess the swans have a wide range of birth dates?

19 June, 2003 *(Denali Nat'l Park)*

Am back in one of my favorite places. Although Denali is nowadays getting a lot of tourist visitors, there is still plenty of backcountry to hike and camp in (and to sometimes get lost in!).

A little rain again. *Enuf already!!*

Photographed a sleeping fox along a creek bottom. It'd wake up and scratch feverously for a minute or so before again nodding off. It was shedding its itchy winter's coat.

Volunteers are pulling dandelions from the first few miles of park road. Dandelions aren't native to the area and they are trying to prevent them from spreading further into the park and overwhelming Denali's native plants. Cars carry the seeds in accidentally on their undersides and tires.

A large beaver crossed the road at mile 8. Likely seeking a new home to homestead.

22 June, 2003 *(Windy Point, south of Anch.)*

A raven chick was fluttering around in the rocks as about 6 adult ravens perched near it or flew around it. Since the chick was already the size of the adults, it was only evident that it was young because some of the others would feed it as it sat squawking with its mouth open. Lambs in the area are getting bigger. Rams have mostly shed their winter's coat but the shaggy ewes still have not. Found only adult marmots near the Whittier tunnel. No young ones out sunning. 65'ish weather.

Spent the afternoon watching a Bald eagles nest in back of Potter Marsh. The two eaglets are getting almost as big looking as the adults. Watched one adult bring back a duck and also a muskrat to the nest. The marsh has all sorts of assorted prey living there and eagles are superb hunters.

Marmot

29 June, 2003 *(Kenai Peninsula)*

Spent the day near a Common loon nest on the Kenai. I knew that the nest was hidden on the shoreline so I just plopped down in the grass and took pictures of the two adults (with a telephoto lens) as they swam nearby every so often.

After a few hours (about 11 AM) I saw the nest-sitting adult come flying off the nest and go into a wild dance of squawking and wing beating. Then I saw that something was moving near the nest and soon caught sight of a mink. I don't think it got any eggs though as the one adult kept charging the area and I soon saw grass moving and the animal evidently leaving. Although the sun was coming into me, I kept shooting. ** Later, after developing, discovered some wonderful "backlit" shots.

I'd love to get a few shots of the chicks riding the backs of the adults later this summer. Might have to pump up the raft for that shoot?

11 December, 2004

Truthfully, I don't know *how this all works*? All I know is that I sense that I feel and see more beauty and awe in Nature than most people probably do. I spend my waking hours spellbound by God's Creation. How could one NOT believe?

Also, I realize that others may not always have the free time or opportunity to travel as I do, so hopefully my art and photographs (and books) will be helpful reference to other artists.

28 December, 2004

First light and *last* light are usually the best time to see wildlife near the roads of Alaska. I always tell tourists to "sleep" during the middle of the day and to drive during the other daylight hours if they want to see animals. Of course this is not always *possible* or *practical*.

4/11 March, 2005 (*Saquaro Nat'l Park, Tucson, AZ*)

Had to head south for a while to gather reference material on Desert bighorns, bobcats, cougars, etc. Working on a Drawing Mammals book.

Spent the past week exploring the desert areas of southern Arizona. Been sunny and warm (80's). Pollen counts are high and the snakes are about. Have seen 4 large rattlesnakes around my campsites and while hiking the backcountry. Not a good idea to put out scattered birdseed near camp (to lure in birds: quail, etc.) as rats and mice would come around to feed on it and the snakes would likely follow this prey. One rattlesnake was truly 5 feet long and could, I believe, take and swallow a cottontail rabbit which are common hereabouts.

Wild flowers are blooming and should soon peak in colors. Southern Arizona had a lot of rain this winter and so the seeds (which often lie dormant if too dry) have sprouted.

Photographed Desert bighorns, coyotes, bobcats, quail and other small animals this past few weeks. Also, did a lot of sketching of desert plants for my reference files. Also, some watercolors to capture the colors of the plants and terrain.

North America is so diverse and spectacular that I often can't decide where my favorite place is. Alaska, however, would still be hard to beat! I do like places with four seasons but from April to September I would probably guess that Alaska is the best place to live. Anchorage, for instance, is usually about 65-70 during most of the summer's months. Perrrrrfect!

Bobcat

4 September, 2005 (*Kodiak notes*)

Took an exciting week trip down to Kodiak Island last week. The salmon are running pretty thick now and so the Kodiak bears are coming down out've the hills to fish for them in the streams. A friend of mine had friends thereabouts who had a very remote cabin in prime bear country and who generously allowed me to use it for the week.

Saturday, August 26th, I caught the morning M/V Kennicott out of Homer for the 9 hour cruise to Kodiak. I had decided on bringing my car on the ferry versus flying down as I had a lot of camera gear as well as odds 'n ends such as a pistol, bear spray, etc. The ferry trip will cost about $450 roundtrip for me/car. My biggest expense will likely be getting to and from the remote cabin.

Mike Druckrey and I were lucky to hitch a boat ride to Kizhuyak bay with Dave Olsen. Dave is Kathy Druckrey's brother and she and Mike own this remote cabin where I am going to stay while photographing bears. After the long boat ride and then shuffling my gear about a mile down the rocky shoreline, Mike and I pulled off the nailed-up boards from the little cabin's door (bear-proofing) before then hiking to a fast-flowing creek to fill up a few water buckets. Later, Mike and I hiked the area to acquaint me with some good sites as well as getting an overall lay of the land. A plane came in later to pick Mike up and fly him back to Kodiak.

The Druckrey's little cabin at the head of Kizhuyak bay.

A view from inside the small cabin. At certain tide-levels one could often see numerous bears fishing or eating sedge-grass.

The next morning I was up early and ready to go hiking. And, although I don't recommend that people travel alone in remote bear country, I nevertheless often do. I followed trails through thick brush much of the day and yelling "Hey Bear, Hey Bear" when stepping around piles of fresh bear scat. I did spook a number of deer but no bears. There are a lot of bears down low on the rivers and I ran into about a dozen during my first day. High tides have stranded a lot of fish along the shores and in the bordering grassy areas and many of the bears seem to be just roaming and scavenging instead of actually fishing the rivers like one usually sees at Brooks Fall or McNeil River in the Katmai area. The adult bears here hardly ever seem to eat the whole fish but rather appear to just peel off and eat the fat-rich skin as well as the eggs of the female salmon. Cubs, however, eat most of Mom's leftovers. Some of the rivers here are literally *boiling with fish* and one surely has to laugh while watching some young bears try to decide exactly *which* fish to chase.

In the mornings I'd climb up on the highest hill and glass the streams and grassy flats below. This would help give me an idea of where the bears were congregating and I could then hike down into the *hottest* spots.

A beautiful sunny day of about 65 degrees. Today, from up high, you could see *forever*. What a wonderful wilderness place this is! It's still surprising and exhilarating at how *alive* one feels when his senses are flooded with the awesome beauty of nature and of clean mountain air. It makes me fondly recall some diary notes I had recorded in one of my books many years ago. Things like, "wilderness air: air so fresh and clean that it's likely never been *used* before". And, "to be the sole owner of all that passes beneath one's feet, unrestrained and unshackled in spirit, that is the true beauty of walking Alaska's wilds". They were notes I had written while living alone in the remote and magnificent Alaska "bush" for a number of winters (upon first arriving in Alaska in 1970) and similar such thoughts filled me now.

This fox followed me around a couple of days. I'm sure it didn't know what I was? If I'd turn my back on him he'd approach to sniff me and to try and nip my boots.

I shot about 6 rolls of film before heading home. At about 11 PM, after a sandwich and hot chocolate, I crawled into my sleeping bag. At about midnight I heard noise but my snoozing mind likely dismissed it as merely a person moving around. Keep on snoozing. Soon, however, a few still-functioning brain cells shouted out: *"Helloooo, you are ALONE in remote bear country*!!! About the time I realized that this noise was a bear, it must've reared up and punched the plywood door with its front paws. BAM! BAM! The whole lil' shack shook and things toppled off the shelves and crashed to the floor. I raised up in bed yelling "HEY!, HEY! at the top of my lungs. Unfortunately, the second "HEY!" didn't make it all the way out as the colorful stars dancing in my head and the excruciating pain of slamming my head into the bed's overhead two-by-four stud caused me to shorten my second "HEY!" to a "H--" and to then follow it with a few colorful expletives. As blood filled my eye socket from the gash, I rolled out of my bag and began beating on the inside of the still bear-shaking flimsy door. I heard the bear stumble or tumble down the steps and, with my powerful halogen light, watched through the window as it casually strolled away down the cabin's trail. After the adult bear disappeared from my light, I fired up the propane lamp, washed out my head gash and bandaged it up with gauze and bandaids from my first-aid kit. Wow, I'll definitely have a wonderful *shiner* for the next few weeks! I might add here that while Mike & Kathy's little cabin is well built, it is only about 8 feet by 8 feet inside and the door has but a small latch on it. Thankfully the thin door opens *out* and not *in* or I'm sure I would've been dancing a polka in my underwear with a 700 pound bear! Also, because of the cabin's small size, the one sleeping area is under a counter that holds the propane camp stove, cooking gear, etc. (I had, incidentally, decided not to cook anything in the cabin because it may attract bears and only used the propane stove to heat up water for washing and for tea/hot chocolate.) There is only about two feet of clearance between ones prone body and the underside of the counter. This counter is also supported by cross two-by-four studs. This "two foot" space is just the *perfect* distance for reaching *maximum* speed (and thus, *maximum head impact*) when jerking upright in bed in the black of the night! Once I got my head bleeding somewhat under control, I found my roll of duct tape (what Alaskan ever leaves home without it?) and taped a few soft towels to the offending two-by-four stud.

About an hour later I finally went back to bed and soon dozed off again. There was now a balanced chair leaned up against the outside of the door and which would hopefully fall and help wake me if another bear came by. Well, at about 3 AM a bear came up the steps and "crash" went my booby-trapped chair. Again I came out of dreamland and yelled "HEY!", "H--!" Luckily I slammed my skull in a new spot and so didn't re-open my previous wound. The taped-up towel also likely prevented another session of blood-letting. Anyhow, with fresh stars dancing in my eyes and a throbbing head, I chased the bear off again. This time I spewed out words I likely haven't used since playing in the jungles of Vietnam, a bunch of years ago. Needless to say I stayed awake the rest of the night.

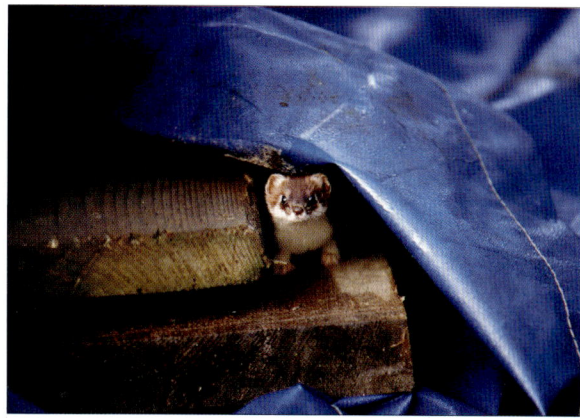

This small weasel (ermine) lived in the woodpile by the cabin. It would run in and out of the cabin if you left the door open for very long. *Very* tame and curious.

** Due to the restrictions of book space I won't be able to detail my day by day activities during this Kodiak adventure. I'll add that weather closed in and my pick-up plane was delayed for an extra day. I did spend 5 exciting days here alone and photographed and watched dozens of bears. Many at very close range near the cabin and on the salmon streams. Some bears would run away upon seeing me and others would just sit down and watch me or walk *towards* me while I fished or photographed them. Those "others" always gave me the willies!

Fishing was also great and I'd hook a pink or silver salmon on nearly every cast. A few fun times were when I was fishing a stream on one side and a bear or two were fishing on the other side. Deer, weasels, eagles and fox were also seen often and showed no fear as most had likely seen few if any humans before. The cooling weather is helping turn the green leaves lighter and yellowish. Autumn will soon be visiting the "Emerald Island" of Kodiak, Alaska. I hope I too will be back visiting again soon.

Also, I've decided to just say: "A Kodiak bear did it!" when people ask me: "What the heck happened to you?" upon viewing my impressive *shiner*. Then, if time permits, I'll tell them the *rest of the story*.....

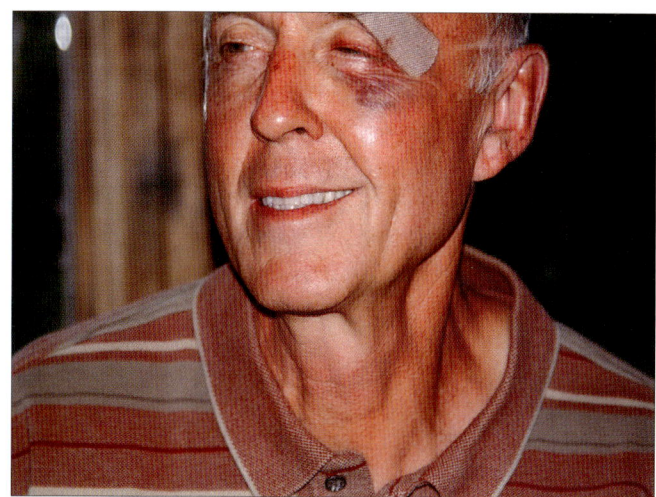

This self-timed photo (unfortunately) missed most of my head injury. Anyhow, it could have been much, much worse if I had actually knocked myself out and the bear entered the cabin.

14 December, 2005 *(Anchorage)*

Making a living in nature photography means you must capture "special moments" in nature and, if you're real lucky, it'll be moments that are pleasing, informative and interesting to viewers of the photos. Personally, I mainly photograph to provide myself with original reference material for my art. However, I am beginning to add more and more photographs to my various books as many viewing artists find the accuracy of a good photograph helpful to them too.

** In 1899, after returning from his first visit to Alaska, geographer Henry Gannett cautioned: "If you are old, go by all means, but if you are young, stay away... The scenery of Alaska is so much grander than anything else in the world... It is not well to dull one's capacity for such enjoyment by seeing the finest first."

27-29 March, 2006 *(Homer, AK)*

Spent a few days in Homer photographing Bald eagles. Jean Keene has been feeding eagles there on the Homer Spit for many years. She often obtains fish and fish scraps from the fish processors during the summer months and keeps it frozen until the "lean" winter months. Oftentimes there are dozens and dozens of eagles perched near her home awaiting the morning fish handout.

Sounds like in a year or two this feeding will end. Jean had been given permission to do it, but now others are beginning to start doing it too, and so it is now being stopped completely.

I once read that over half of the Bald eagle photographs published in books and magazines in the past 10 years have come from photographers shooting eagles here on the Homer Spit. In fact, the Stock Agency that I sell my photographs through is not accepting anymore Bald eagle photos as their inventory is so full of them.

Bald Eagles/Homer

8 April, 2006 *(Anchorage)*

Just read that two Anchorage men have been accused by the state of poaching Dall sheep rams in Chugach State Park south of Anchorage. I sure hope they "hang" if found guilty. To kill these magnificent animals that are so easily viewed by all us residents and tourists is truly unforgivable.

I'm sure I hung out with these two rams many times while up in the mountains photographing them. They were so used to people and hikers that to shoot them would've been like shooting fish in a barrel. And, in a State Park that is closed to hunting. *Real sportsmen*, hey?

26-28 April, 2006 *(Cantwell area)*

Spent a few days working on a movie with the Alaska Wildlife Conservation Center. The movie, due out in 2007, is a Sean Penn directed movie called "Into The Wild". It is a story of a young man who came to Alaska and ended up starving to death in an old deserted school bus in the Alaska wilderness. He had kept a journal and the movie used it (and a popular published book) to produce this movie.

The movie had a mother caribou and calf in it (from AWCC) and I volunteered to help with them; leading them into the backcountry on a leash and then making them come to food (off their leash and with me out of the camera view) during the filming. Also helped with some of the other animals.

Was really a fun few days watching how movies are made. It was easy to see that it can take a lot of money to hire all the people needed to get the gear into the wilderness. Am anxious to see the finished movie and see how all the little pieces got put together.

10 May, 2006 *(S. of Anchorage)*

Dozens of Bald eagles and gulls fishing for hooligan (small smelt-like fish) that are migrating along the Turnagain Arm shoreline. Also, dozens of fishermen using nets to scoop them up as they pass by. 20 Mile river is a hot spot.

Arctic terns, grebes, gulls and other shorebirds are busily establishing nesting territories around Southcentral Alaska. Sunny and 60's these past few days. Beautiful.

Arctic Tern

16 May, 2006 *(Trip to Fairbanks)*

Cool spring weather this year, birch leaves are just beginning to bud out. Lakes are pretty much broken-up but some lake "bays" are still ice-covered. Still some snow in certain areas on my drive North from Anchorage. A few swans and pintail ducks are swimming in the open ponds.

Spent a little time in Denali Nat'l Park. The creeks and rivers there are running fast and muddy from the rapid snow melt. Seeing a lot of Snowshoe hares that are still mostly white and they are very conspicuous in areas where there is no snow to camouflage themselves from predators.

Fairbanks has had some 60 degree days and no freezing nights and hence it seems "greener" than "cooler" Anchorage was.

20 May, 2006 *(Valdez area)*

Thompson Pass still has a lot of snow. Male ptarmigan are still mostly white hereabouts but they are busy establishing and protecting their nesting territories from other intruding males. Always fun to watch their aerial dog-fights.

Spotted a Mountain goat bedded in the woods near Mile 19 of the Valdez Hwy. It had fallen from the rocks (according to fish & game) and struck its head, breaking a horn and possibly injuring an eye. It was still there a few days later on my return trip and I heard later that it had to be destroyed due to its injuries. They, more than any other large mammal, live in such steep and hazardous country that falls and avalanches likely claim a number of them. Predators, however, are few. Even bears have been killed by the sharp, dagger-like horns of the male and female goats.

25 May, 2006 *(Kenai)*

Watched a cow moose give birth today. First time I have actually seen the calf "fall". After the cow licked the calf clean, it tried to stand but couldn't. Its legs were *like rubber*. Finally, it stood for a moment before tumbling into the nearby pond. Poor little guy almost drowned before it could right itself and get its head up out of the water.

The light was "backlit", so not sure how my photos will turn out. But, sure was fun to watch this little drama unfold. And with only me to witness.

Cow Moose With Calf

3 June, 2006 (Girdwood)

A lot of wildflowers (especially lupines) growing along the roadsides of Alaska now.

First baby goslings spotted at Potter Marsh. Sunny and very windy along the ocean's shoreline. A lot of ice has broken off of Portage Glacier and is floating in Portage lake. This glacier, incidentally, has "retreated" a few miles over the past 10 years or so. Too bad, as it had been one of the major tourist destinations here in southcentral Alaska.

Also, the Great Horned owl chicks are already gone from their nest on a cliffside along the Matanuska river outside of Palmer, Alaska. *Strange*? Too early.

Portage Lake

21 June, 2006 (Windy Point)

Followed 13 mature Dall ewes along their trails near Windy Point (s. of Anchorage). None of them had lambs. A bad sign. Predators? Or the rash of poaching of big rams that has been occurring in the area may have eliminated the most dominant and productive breeding stock? Anyhow, it was a *sad sight* for a nature lover.

4/6 October, 2006 (Kenai River)

Went fishing with Jim Patka for a few days on the Kenai river. Jim and Terry have a cabin on the river and we went down there to winterize it and the boat. But, of course, we fished a few days first. It was cold and there was ice on the river's edge during the morning hours.

We caught Silver salmon, rainbows and dollies. We released the dollies and rainbows but kept a few salmon to eat. Was a few days of peacefully drifting up and down the river. Only a dozen or so other boats around; mainly guides fishing with their clients.

10 October, 2006 (Anchorage)

Preparing for a winter of painting. Have mainly been illustrating books for the past decade and have decided to try some "oils" this winter. Most of my formal art education was in the fine arts and therefore did a lot of oils. However, when I moved to Alaska I began to do more pencil sketches and watercolors because they were easier to transport in the small bush planes that flew me in and out of my remote cabins and homes.

This "change" is very exciting to me and I am looking forward to a great winter of skiing and painting here in Alaska. Let the snow fall!

11 November, 2006 (Bird Creek area)

Photographed a Hawk owl that was hunting shrews/voles along the Seward highway this morning. Was able to approach quite close without alarming it.

Hawk owls used to be a commonly seen owl hereabouts but I have seen very few of them these past few years. *Not sure why?*

19 April, 2007 (Denali Nat'l Park)

The first 30 miles of road are open to traffic prior to the tour buses beginning their summer schedules. Only spent two days and didn't see much for wildlife except some scattered bands of caribou. There was, however, a lot of hair-filled wolf scat scattered about on the road between mileposts 8 and 12, indicating that they likely used the road for movement from, to, or during their hunts.

Partly sunny during the days and cold at night. Did tent camp outside the park and it probably dropped down to 15-20 degrees at night. Double sleeping bag weather!

Was able to ski into certain areas but overall the best backcountry skiing is over for the Spring. Had hoped that the hare population would still be high and would therefore ignite higher predator numbers. However, I didn't see many hares in the area. The male Willow ptarmigan were just starting to establish their nesting territories and a few aerial dog-fights amongst males were sighted. Another week or so will be better for close-up ptarmigan photography as the males will then often be perched on tall lookout trees within their established territory and are usually easily approached.

Author at Campsite

2 May, 2007 (Palmer area)

A cute Alaskan joke. An Alaskan boy was visiting down south and got into a bragging discussion with two other young boys about their fathers. One boy bragged that his dad smoked "crack". The other boy bragged that his dad smoked "weed". The Alaskan boy, who also wanted to brag up his dad but knew he didn't smoke crack or pot, finally blurted out, "my dad smokes, ahhhhhhhh, FISH!" ☺

5 June, 2007 (McHugh Creek)

Cow moose with twin calves are hanging out south of McHugh Creek. Did notice that the cow had porcupine quills in at least one leg and did find a "squished" porkie nearby. Evidently momma moose stomped it. Wonder how that whole scene played-out?

7/8 June, 2007 (Potter Marsh area)

Have been watching a Great Horned owl's nest with two chicks in it the past few days. It is located on the eastside of Potter Marsh and it appears that the owls had taken over an abandoned raven's nest. Chicks are growing fast and are beginning to flap their wings and fluttering around the tree limbs. Watched an adult owl feed them a squirrel last Sunday and watched as one chick swallowed a piece of the squirrel with its long, furry tail still attached. Gulp!

Mallard ducklings and Canada geese goslings are being born this past week or so.

**Owl chicks left their nest on June 10th. Owls and ravens are usually early nesters. A lot of Bald eagles along Turnagain Arm, must still be a lot of hooligan fish migrating through.

26 June, 2007 (Clear Creek/Talkeetna area)

Rich & Betty Gorr and Charlie & Sharon Frank came up for an Alaska vacation. Rich, Charlie (both Minnesota school friends) and I boated into Clear Creek (up by Talkeetna) for a day of guided King salmon fishing. A lot of fun and we caught about 8 kings which we released. Our chuckle of the day was when poor Rich got pooped on by an eagle that had landed in a tall cottonwood tree above him. That poop had to have fallen 50 feet before it splattered on his head. Guess it was pretty rank stuff!

27th & 28th: Fished the Kenai and Kasilof rivers with our friend Jay Sjogren. Picked up a few Kings. Rich called a few days later to tell me he had caught a 100# plus halibut on a charter out of Anchor Point. Rich & Betty went home with a lot of pounds of fish but I don't think Charlie and Sharon brought any home? Of course Charlie fishes a lot in Georgia.

4-8 July, 2007 (*McNeil River*)

Exciting few days watching and photographing bears at McNeil River and Mikfik Creek. These are some of the premier bear-viewing areas in Alaska and you have to be selected via a state run lottery. Only 10 people per day are allowed into the refuge. You get there via an hour flight out of Homer, Alaska.

Saw a lot of bears. It was a little early for the Chum salmon run at McNeil River (mid-July is normally the "peak") and so the bears weren't "stacked up" at the best fishing spots yet. We did, however, see at least 20 bears every day and many at very, very close range. We were required to stay close together in a group and had no bear trouble. We did travel with a different Fish & Game guy every day who carried a shotgun but none of them has ever had to use it.

We hiked most of the day around the area. Hip boots are necessary as you often have to cross streams and muddy areas. We'd return home as the changing tides required. In the mornings it was common to find fresh bear poop around our tents, indicating that the bears were certainly in camp during the dark evening hours.

My favorite photography part of the trip was shooting a sow with two cubs that were often riding her back as she fed on the sedge. Until the salmon become more plentiful, the sows with new cubs will likely stay away from the river spots where the large boars are fishing. Later on, when the salmon runs are peaking, fish can be caught all along the river and away from the dangerous big males. Unfortunately, one young cub did get too far away from its protective Mom and did get caught by another bear. ☹

On our last day I did get some photographs of a Red fox returning to its den with a ground squirrel. Also got a few quick shots of the young fox kits peeking out of the safety of their holes.

This trip is an *amazing* Alaska adventure and I'd recommend it for most people. There are a few miles of walking each day (some through streams and mud) but it is doable for most people. *Sadly*, I can't apply again for two years.

Since the *peak* of the salmon run had not yet arrived, the younger bears would spend much of their day just playing or wrestling with siblings or other young bears.

Young bears are extremely playful.

A young fox kit peeks out of the bushes near one of the entrance holes to its den.

We were required to stay in the tight group and not wander apart. Keith Richards of Australia takes pictures of a passing male and female bear while our Fish & Game guide, Doug Hill, looks on.

This sow and spring cubs were seen most everyday near our camp. Mother bears with new cubs would stay off by themselves and not get near other bears that could possibly threaten them. However, few bears are foolish enough to get too near these *very protective* and *aggressive* "moms".

A large male bear fishing at McNeil Falls.

Visits to the camp outhouse (especially nighttime!) can be a little *spooky!*

Nan Elliot, one of the daily permit holders, persuades a curious bear to leave our tenting area. It was not unusual to wake up in the mornings and find bear scat outside our tents.

This sow often had one or two young cubs riding her back while she fed in the tall sedge grass. We never saw this family do any fishing; just fed on vegetation.

27 July, 2007 (Valdez/Copper Center area)

Did a little fishing in the area. Still a little early for Silver salmon this year. Did take a cruise and saw a lot of Sea otters, whales and sea lions. Also delivered some "originals" along the drive. Gas is about $3.20 per gallon hereabouts. Fireweed, incidentally, usually is at its best from July 20-28 in the Valdez area.

Also, while I was at Bayside RV park, Deb Hansen discovered a young elephant seal (*very rare* in Alaska) that had swam up a small drainage ditch near their properties edge. She called the Alaska SeaLife Center in Seward and Tim Lebling and Nikki Dinsmore came to rescue it. They surmised that food, climate or water temperatures may have been the cause for this and a few other elephant seals to be this far North. It will be kept at the SeaLife Center until its skin irritation heals up and it can be released back into the wild.

2 September, 2007 (Anch./Girdwood)

Bull moose are just beginning to shed their "velvet" in the Anchorage/Girdwood area. They should begin sparring with one another in a week or so? Hope I can find some good big bull-battles this year. A friend, Gary Lackie, showed me some good moose spots in Kincaid Park.

Photographer Gary Lackie

6 September, 2007 (Anchorage)

Down to my last 3 rolls of film. Must keep a "restrained" trigger-finger until my film order arrives. Guess I am one of the few "pro's" still shooting film. Will likely switch to digital this winter? I did say *that* last winter but a bad fall (in a basketball game) and a resulting head fracture/concussion took care of most of that winter. Took me about four full months to finally shake the vertigo and bad headaches. Therefore got very little artwork done last winter; only completed about 6 oils from October to December (before the injury).

Below is the first painting completed *after* my head injury. *What the……..?*

"Wild Ram"

23 September, 2007 (Anchorage area)

Rainy and upper 40's. "Termination dust" (snow) on the mountain tops. Swans and geese are flying overhead, pointing south. Hoping for no wind as the bright autumn colors are going to peak soon. Photographing moose (who are beginning to bunch up for the rut) in Kincaid park and Powerline Pass.

Was driving south towards Portage when I saw 17 swans circling above Potter Marsh. By the time I got pulled over they had just landed. 10 seconds earlier and I could have caught them flying against the yellowish-colored hillsides. "Getting a great shot" often simply means being in the *right place at the right time*. Then, just point, shoot and pray…

Snow Blankets the High Country

8 November, 2007 (Portage/Girdwood area)

About a hundred swans flew down the Portage Valley early this afternoon. Imagine they are heading through the Pass and then working their way towards Vancouver area? Got a few aerial shots with nice mountain backgrounds. Most of the ponds are mostly frozen hereabouts (past few days) and so they have to keep moving south.

Did chase a few hares around the brush. Tough to get them out into the open for clean "shots". They are now almost pure white and hence quite noticeable. They are probably "sittin' ducks" for the eagles, owls and other predators that can easily spot them now here in this still snowless landscape. They are, however, seemingly more wary now that their usual camouflage doesn't protect them.

21 November, 2007 (Girdwood)

Read an article that stated that there are an estimated 350 Black bears and 50 Grizzly bears living in the Anchorage "bowl"; an area from Euklutna to Girdwood. Smokes! That is a lot of bears!

23 November 2007

Running into a big problem here with this new twelfth Sketchbook edition. Am using a new printer in Korea and am unable to retrieve any of my older film negatives from another overseas printer. My previous Sketchbook editions were all set-up and printed via film and it now has to be converted digitally for today's usage. Unfortunately I no longer have access to my original art, etc. and so we had to re-shoot nearly all my art directly from previous books and also retype or scan all the text. And, since printing is done via "dots", all the new scans had to be slightly "tweaked out of focus" to overcome the problems of reprinting an existing dot pattern. Hopefully the art won't appear "too" fuzzy! Fingers crossed…

AND SO ENDS MY "JOURNAL". As I've mentioned previously, I have tried to record only that which I thought applied to my life as a lover of nature, artist and photographer, and what I saw through the eyes of a man in this pursuit.

This journal was not professionally edited and was typeset exactly as my notes read. Therefore all grammatical errors are mine alone. Since this "Sketchbook" is a very "personal thing" (a one-man's effort) I felt that I'd rather have my notes recorded exactly as I had written them than of having them rewritten, improved and corrected by someone else.

So, wishing y'all "happy trails and good mushing"!

"**Into the Wild**". This is one of three limited-edition giclee prints that the artist did to celebrate Alaska's (the 49th State) 49th anniversary (1959-2008). The other two are "**Triple Trouble**" (p. 128) and "**Denali Country**" (p. 224).

"Denali Country"

    Alaska is a land of Polar bears, Tlingit Indians, towering mountains, and dazzling fields of fireweed. Land of 375,000,000 acres; of "midnight suns"; of almost unbelievably cold winter temperatures. A land of riches; of oil, gold, timber and fish.

    Alaska is a land of untold wealth and indescribable beauty, and yet (and perhaps mainly because of it) a land with giant problems. Federal interference, ecological battles, Native rights, exploitation, and even foreign fishermen are but a handful of this new state's worries. Alaska has become a battleground for local and national organizations who are concerned not only with its welfare but their own as well. It is a place that often wishes to be left alone and not be mettled with by "good-do'ers" from around the world. Alaskans are a proud group of people who want to decide their own fate.

    The 49th state of America, then, is a state of conflict, of turmoil, of change. Immutable it is not. "North to the Future" is a common bumper-sticker; high rise buildings (built with earthquakes in mind) are no longer uncommon and caribou and moose numbers are presently very low. The oil companies have moved in with their big money, people and machinery and have, in a very short period, changed the state and its people. There is truly a different "attitude" in Alaska today than there was in the pre-Trans-Alaskan pipeline days. "Progress" has arrived at our shores. No longer is Alaska the north country of yesteryear.

    And yet I think there is hope for those of us who loved this "north country of yesteryear" and call this place "home". Alaska is still a state of long winter nights, of frigid temperatures, of mosquitoes, and of a somewhat frontier atmosphere. Perhaps when the oil pipeline has run its course or when energy-hungry America has evolved to a new energy source, Alaska can finally again relax and go back to its former pace. Already I feel nostalgic.

    And so it is, this Far North country of ice and snow and awesome beauty that I came to some years back and have since settled "forever" in. It is still a place where a man can be free, to have some elbow-room to move around in. A place where one can walk "to the beat of his own drums". A place where great herds of mammals still roam and where the "whoosh" of the wings of thousands of birds can still at times be heard overhead. A place where tiny mountain flowers still sway in gentle summer winds.

    I remember my first glimpse of Alaska. I vividly remember looking out of the window of a military airliner and seeing a small cabin on the edge of a lake with a thin, straight column of chimney smoke rising above it. And I remember thinking of it as I spent a year in the jungles of Vietnam and later while finishing college in Minnesota. It is one of my fondest memories in life and I am happy to say that it is now the life I live. I am now that person building that fire in that lakeside wilderness cabin. And I am at peace with myself.

**Journal entry from 5 / 12 / 1981

Doug Lindstrand
Alaska